The Grace of Giving

BY THE SAME AUTHOR . . .

Heart Cry for Revival
I'll Take the High Road

The Grace of Giving

Thoughts On Financial Stewardship

Stephen Olford

ZONDERVAN
PUBLISHING HOUSE

OF THE ZONDERVAN CORPORATION
GRAND RAPIDS, MICHIGAN 49506

THE GRACE OF GIVING
Copyright © 1972 by The Zondervan Corporation Grand Rapids, Michigan
Second printing 1974
Library of Congress Catalog Card Number 72-83872

Printed in the United States of America

DEDICATION

To the members of Calvary Baptist Church, from whom I have learned much concerning *The Grace of Giving,* and with whom I have had "fellowship in the gospel," I affectionately dedicate this book.

CONTENTS

Foreword

Preface

Introduction 13

1. The Basis of Blessing 27

2. The Essentiality of Giving 37

3. The Example of Giving 47

4. The Ethics of Giving 57

5. The Efficiency of Giving 69

6. The Enrichment of Giving 81

7. The Maintenance of the Ministry . . . 97

Conclusion 111

Appendix 123

References 132

Bibliography 137

FOREWORD

Christians everywhere stand in need of clear instruction in the principles that govern the proper use of money. To a large degree the use of money for Christian causes is either exploited or neglected altogether because of such abuses. Our Lord's own teaching regarding money and earthly possessions is a refreshing contrast to the distorted concepts that too frequently have blurred the vision of the church and robbed its members of the "grace of giving." He completely lifted the concept of earthly possessions to the eternal realm of treasure in heaven.

Those matchless parables told by the Lord Jesus have affected the attitudes and even the vocabulary of the civilized world. Everyone thinks of a "Samaritan" in terms of the story of the "Good Samaritan." When speaking of the true meaning and value of money, the Lord used parables with incisive effect. It would be profitable to remind ourselves of one of these parables and the result.

> And he said also unto his disciples, There was a certain rich man, which had a steward; and the same was accused unto him that he had wasted his goods. And he called him, and said unto him, How is it that I hear this of thee? give an account of thy stewardship; for thou mayest be no longer steward.
> Then the steward said within himself, What shall I do? for my lord taketh away from me the stewardship: I cannot dig; to beg I am ashamed. I am resolved what to do, that, when I am put out of the stewardship, they may receive me into their houses.
> So he called every one of his lord's debtors unto

him, and said unto the first, How much owest thou unto my lord? And he said, A hundred measures of oil. And he said unto him, Take thy bill, and sit down quickly, and write fifty.

Then said he to another, And how much owest thou? And he said, A hundred measures of wheat. And he said unto him, Take thy bill, and write fourscore.

And the lord commended the unjust steward, because he had done wisely: for the children of this world are in their generation wiser than the children of light.

And I say unto you, Make to yourselves friends of the mammon of unrighteousness; that, when ye fail, they may receive you into everlasting habitations. He that is faithful in that which is least is faithful also in much: and he that is unjust in the least is unjust also in much. If therefore ye have not been faithful in the unrighteous mammon, who will commit to your trust the true riches? And if ye have not been faithful in that which is another man's, who shall give you that which is your own?

No servant can serve two masters: for either he will hate the one, and love the other; or else he will hold to the one, and despise the other. Ye cannot serve God and mammon.

And the Pharisees also, who were covetous, heard all these things: and they derided him (Luke 16:1-14).

The master of this unjust steward did not commend him because he was unjust in the way he handled his master's money, but because he had used this money shrewdly from the standpoint of what would be to his own best advantage. In commenting upon His own story, our Lord challenges Christians by the example of this unrighteous steward, who shows such prudence in the things of the world: "For the children of this world are in their generation wiser than the children of light." Or, in the words of another: "The children of the world show more sense in material things than

Christians show in spiritual things." If our money can be so used to gain eternal riches, not only for ourselves but for others who shall receive us into "everlasting habitations," then the only wise use of our possessions is that all be given to God. Money is for one purpose — to give to God. It is in this connection that we can understand the reference to the giving of the Corinthian Christians described in the statement, "First, they gave their own selves to the Lord." Even when using money for human needs they were using that money for God, inasmuch as they had first given themselves to the Lord. Practically speaking, the way of the Lord is that money should be used for personal and family needs and the rest is to be invested in eternal things. Like the covetous Pharisees, most of us shrink from this and try vainly to live for two masters. Yet, to be free from covetousness would mean that we should be free from all anxiety about earthly things.

The author of *The Grace of Giving* writes as a pastor, recognizing that the members of a local congregation have a responsibility to give systematically to the full support of the church that maintains a living ministry in the power of the Holy Spirit. The principles set forth in *The Grace of Giving* will enrich the life of the Christian who walks in them with his Lord, and will vitally contribute to the furtherance of Christian work everywhere.

G. ALLEN FLEECE, D.D.

PREFACE

In commending *The Grace of Giving* to the prayerful perusal of you, my reader, I must acknowledge, with gratitude, the advice and assistance that I have derived from the authors named in these pages; the counsel and suggestions from Dr. J. C. Macaulay, my colleague and theological consultant; and the inspiration from my congregation to whom I have dedicated this book. I also want to thank my dear friend, Dr. G. Allen Fleece, for writing the Foreword. Then, as always, my warm appreciation goes to Miss Victoria Kuhl who has typed and prepared the manuscript for publication.

All this teamwork will have been more than worthwhile if, through the reading of this book the God of giving reproduces in us The Grace of Giving to His eternal glory and the spread of the Gospel to the ends of the earth.

STEPHEN F. OLFORD, D.D., LITT.D.
Calvary Baptist Church
New York City

INTRODUCTION

The story is told of a circus athlete who earned his living by displaying astonishing feats of physical strength. His "show" would normally conclude with a simple, but impressive, demonstration of his ability to squeeze an orange dry! After completing his act, he would then challenge his audience to produce anyone who could extract even one drop of juice from the crushed fruit.

On one of these occasions, a little man volunteered. He was so diminutive that his very appearance raised a laugh from the spectators. Undaunted, however, the man stepped onto the stage and took from the athlete what appeared to be nothing more than a shriveled up piece of rind. Then, bracing himself, he slowly and firmly compressed his right hand. Every eye was on him, and the atmosphere was electric! A moment or two elapsed, and then, to everyone's amazement — and not least the athlete — a drop of orange juice formed and dripped to the floor. As the cheers subsided, the athlete beckoned the man forward, asked his name, and then invited him to tell the crowd how he had managed to develop such fistic powers. "Nothing to it," replied the man; and then, with a grin, he added: "I happen to be the treasurer of the local Baptist Church!"

There was a time when I thought that the foregoing was a good "offertory" joke; but this is no longer the case. As a pastor and preacher I have come to see that *consecrated and consistent giving* never result from arm-twisting and browbeating appeals. Now and again such methods might work, but in the long run they are doomed to failure.

Perhaps my convictions are best expressed in some paragraphs that appeared a few years ago in what was then known as *The Sunday School Times*:

"Competition for the Christian's dollar among churches, religious organizations, and other benevolent groups is conducted on a level today that removes giving from the area of a spiritual grace. A Wisconsin State College history professor made a telling point when he concluded in his study of Protestant giving that the doctrine of stewardship has not 'had much to do with actual human motivation at either the level of promotion or the level of giving.'

"If evangelicals do have a theology of stewardship and giving, it is difficult to recognize it in their efforts to raise money — efforts which range all the way from a super-pious 'this is a faith work' to the more crass 'I'm doing you a favor to relieve you of some of your money.' Since believers are bombarded with appeals through the mail, from the pulpit, at banquets, and over the radio, how can they be expected to arrive at any Scriptural view of giving?

"The local church and nonchurch related works must bear much of the blame for this deplorable state of affairs. If believers are not taught a Scriptural doctrine of stewardship, can they be expected to give intelligently and can they be expected to realize that giving is indeed as vital a spiritual ministry as witnessing, reading the Bible, and praying?

"If the appeals are based on the techniques of modern advertising and selling, will not the response be the same? Hence, the glamorous, the emotional, the 'squeaking wheel' type of promotion gets the best response. Fund raising has become a science with 'proven' results. Where is the work of God the Holy Spirit in this? How does the believer come to know the blessed thrill of his gift becoming 'an odour of a sweet smell, a sacrifice acceptable, wellpleasing unto God' (Phil. 4:18)?

14

"On the other hand, Christians must understand that they cannot excuse themselves from giving just because much of the technique of fund raising does not measure up to Scriptural standards. There is no excuse for not giving. But giving must be in response to the promptings of the Holy Spirit, which may or may not come through an appeal letter or a desperate pulpit or radio plea.

"The solution ought never to be one of expedience to achieve the desired goal. If it seems that Christians are not giving as much as they should, this is no reason for financial appeals to degenerate to the methods of modern salesmanship. If a person resents emotional, long-winded appeals, this is no reason for him not to give. Asker and giver ought to be motivated by that which is completely in harmony with the example of Scripture. The Apostle Paul was not embarrassed to write of his needs. He reminded the churches of their duty to give, but he never resorted to begging. . . . He taught that giving was indeed a spiritual sacrifice that brought fruit to the account of those who gave."[1]

In common with the author of this editorial, I discovered from the study of the New Testament that the divine concept of giving is that it is a *grace*; hence the title of this book — *The Grace of Giving* (see Chapter 3 on The Example of Giving).

With this new insight, I prepared a series of expository sermons which I delivered to my congregation. This, incidentally, accounts for the structure and style of my presentation throughout these chapters. Now preaching on stewardship is not usually acceptable under general circumstances; but my misgivings during the weeks that followed were totally unfounded! The giving in the church improved immediately. But more important than this was the transforming effect of this ministry on the members, friends and guests who ex-

---

[1] 1962, p. 455

posed themselves to this doctrine of *The Grace of Giving*.

Among the many letters I received from people in the congregation, and listeners to our broadcasts, are five which I have chosen to include in this Introduction to my book. I have selected these because they are so typical of those who urged me to publish these sermons for the edification and encouragement of a wider Christian public.

There was one from a church member who had some initial doubts about an entire series on giving. She wrote:

"One of the greatest blessings I received from your messages on tithing was that of the emphasis on the *teaching* of the whole Word of God on the subject. So many of the verses have come back to me again and again: 'Bring ye all the tithes . . . and prove me now, saith the Lord'; 'Let everyone of you lay by in store as God hath prospered him'; 'Providing things honest in the sight of all men'; 'Let all things be done decently and in order'; the 'firstfruits of all thine increase.'

"I also realize more fully that the Lord is a God of order. He says 'to lay by in store' on payday. God is infinitely more real when we put money in an envelope for Him. God is interested in the material needs of our lives. He has kept me from wasting money, and helped me to hold more closely to a budget. He has provided also in other ways, in lovely things that have come to me from people that knew nothing of the situation, tokens of His love and His presence with me.

"I believe order in money is tied up with order in our whole lives; there is something deep within us connected with money; we spend our lives either getting or preparing to earn money, and it seems reasonable that God who 'giveth us the strength to get wealth' should be interested in how we use it.

"He is interested in how we use our tithe; there are many places where we could give it, many causes that are needy and faithful to the Lord. I believe we should seek His guidance in giving our tithe. I believe we should support the places where we ourselves receive help; we need a true attitude about poverty and Christian works; God's faithful servants are 'worthy of their hire.' There is a reciprocity to life! I feel we should share something of what we have in this world also with the poor, and that we should support faithful missionaries who cannot use their time or their strength to earn money, but who spend their lives and even hazard them for the Lord.

"All these things have gone through my mind so very much since you spoke on this subject. I feel there is so much more to learn and to do. We have to go back to Him so often. Perhaps that is why we need this little book."

Another testimony was shared by a former Dean of Women, and distinguished Bible teacher, who is being used greatly in home study circles in New York City. She observed that "giving as a grace was a new thought to me. I have never heard such a helpful series of messages on the subject. They turn the basis for giving completely away from any thought of legalism to total grace; from compulsion to joyous cooperation with Him, who for our sakes 'became poor' in His self-giving.

"Many years ago I saw that Christians had not really *given* anything to God until they had given beyond the tithe which He rightfully claims as His own. I had always believed that what I gave with a pure motive would be rewarded. But the teaching of the present 'enrichment of giving' — that 'the grace of giving is God's supreme method of enriching,' both to the giver and the receiver, and that giving increases our capacity for receiving deep spiritual enrichment have been blessed truths indeed!

"Surely Christians who receive this teaching into their hearts will be eternally grateful to you. What a glory would come to God, what enrichment to the givers, and what growth to the work of the Lord, if such messages were given in every church! There would be no missionaries waiting for funds to go out to the field, and no financial problems in the home church, if Christians viewed giving in this light. May the love of God move us to give in pure worship of Him who gave His life a ransom for many!"

Then there were some comments submitted by no less a person than a Christian economist! Times without number he has advised the officers of our church on wise stewardship. As he listened to the sermons on *The Grace of Giving* he recalled "many reminiscences," then added: "I thought of a man of great and widespread influence who, when I knew him many years ago, used to consider such money as he had as not really his, but only in his keeping as God's steward. I heard him tell that when he was a young boy, on some special occasion, he had received as a present a 'double eagle' (a twenty dollar gold piece), a very large sum to him at that time. He went to a church service and when a collection was taken for foreign missions he put the double eagle in the plate. Although I think that he was not applauded for this at home, afterward he told how much the sense of 'having given all' meant to him.

"In a book published nearly forty years ago, Bruce Barton told of a man, 'another St. Francis,' who had worked all his life among the poorest of a great city. When asked how he lived in view of the fact that he gave all his little income away, he said that he had an 'assurance of income,' a 'promissory note signed by the Owner of the universe.' This was the note: 'Trust in the Lord, and do good; so shalt thou dwell in the land, and verily thou shalt be fed.'

"The very word 'tithing' makes me think of my parents. Tithing was just a beginning with my father, who was a minister with the modest minister's salary of that period. Yet in the depression years it was they who were able to keep the children (from our church) in the country, during the long summer months. I have never forgotten how once, when talking to my father about settling up for his expenses, and he had demurred at the smallness of the sum, that he finally said, 'Well, you see, it was a real pleasure for us to have them.'

"Personal income being what it is today, it is not necessary even to use pencil and paper to see what tithing would do for the financial problems of churches in general if everyone tithed."

A further letter came from a minister who, before assuming his own pastorate, spent a number of years visiting churches across the country expounding such themes as holiness, revival, stewardship and evangelism. Fully aware, therefore, of the current needs and trends in religious circles, he maintained that "there is certainly a need today for a clear, biblical exposition on this all-important subject of 'Christian Giving.' All too often 'giving' has become the occasion for an emotional, high-pressure appeal, largely concerned with the financial response — and lacking in the moral, spiritual and biblical aspects of a subject clearly set forth in the Scriptures as the God-appointed ministry of every Christian.

"You have presented these messages with a faithfulness and dignity that elevates this entire subject to its rightful place. 'The Enrichment of Giving' is a message that was of particular blessing to me, and one that should be read and re-read until it is written deep in the heart of every child of God. It is many years since I accepted the Lordship of Christ with regard to my money and these messages have challenged me afresh on stewardship. They have brought a new desire to serve the Lord with the material resources that so vitally affect the outreach of the gospel to our generation.

"The church and people that give heed to these

messages will surely find not only a new liberality to meet every need, but a new joy in the ministry of giving that will be in itself a witness to the power of Christ to save from sin and inbred selfishness."

The last communication was from someone very special. Before his home-call he was a member of Calvary Baptist Church for over forty years. During that time he served on many boards and committees; and throughout the period I knew him he was the treasurer of our entire operation and outreach. With brevity, and yet significant comprehensiveness, he expressed himself in the following manner:

"I have been treasurer for some years, and concerned with the budget and the methods of meeting it. After you delivered these sermons there was a noticeable increase in the giving of the church. It became my joy not only to see budgetary needs met, but the blessing of the Lord upon the work, as our people followed the commands of Christ.

"Although we have long been familiar with the idea of tithing, many people have never realized how much a part of worship giving actually is. I join with you in the earnest hope that readers of this book will grasp the depth of this teaching for the first time."

It is because of these expressions of encouragement that I address myself to readers across this land and, please God, beyond these United States of America. As you peruse these pages you will observe a threefold treatment of our subject.

First of all, there is *the basis of giving*. This is dealt with in the first chapter, and is based upon an Old Testament passage (Mal. 3:7-15). The fact that it is Old Testament must not turn you off! Remember "that the Old Testament is the New Testament concealed, and the New Testament is the Old Testament revealed!" The Bible which contains both Old and New Testaments *is the Word of God*. The burden of this particular passage is this matter of the *tithe* — and I hasten to add that tithing was not only an Old Testament principle and practice. The late Tom Rees, in his little book *Money Talks,* reminds us that "the early church according to Origen, Jerome and Chrysostom, following the example and teaching of our Lord and the Apostles, both taught and practiced tithing.

"Students of Church History tell us that tithing has been practiced widely in the Christian Church since New Testament days.

"Tithes were recognized legally in England as early as A.D. 786, and tithing was a common practice during the reigns of Alfred, Edgar, and Canute.

"The Council of Trent (1545) not only enjoined payment of tithes but went so far as to excommunicate those who withheld them!

"The principle of tithing is timeless. It is for every man in every age and dispensation. It was neither instituted by the dispensation of law nor terminated by the dispensation of grace. It was neither given by Moses nor abrogated by Jesus Christ.

"Tithing was both incorporated into the Law of Moses and into the New Testament Church.

"The principle of the Sabbath is similar to that of tithing.

"The Sabbath was given by God and practiced by man from the Creation. In every age God has demanded one-seventh of man's time. This timeless principle was not first given with the Law of Moses. It was, however, incorporated into that Law. The wording of the fourth commandment reminds us of this: 'Remember the Sabbath day, to keep it holy' (Exod. 20:8). Later, this same principle of one day in seven was by common consent adopted by the New Testament church.

"The Lord's day and the Lord's tithe stand or fall together. The New Testament assumes that all enlightened and obedient Christians will both set aside at

21

least one-seventh of their time and one-tenth of their income for the Lord.

"Yes, thank God, we 'are not under the law, but under grace' (Rom. 6:14); therefore the giving of our money and time is no longer a matter of legality and bondage, but rather of privilege and joyful experience.

"If the Hebrews, compelled by Law, gave one-tenth, how can we, constrained by Grace, give one mite less? 'What then? Shall we sin, because we are not under the law, but under grace? God forbid'. . . . Love is the fulfilling of the law' (Rom. 6:15, 13:10)."[2]

Secondly, there are *the barriers of giving*. Here, I am reminded of the opening words of an article by Dr. J. C. Macaulay entitled "Men Ought to Give." In his characteristic style he writes: "The preacher's sermon, according to established custom, had three points: 1) Make all you can; 2) Save all you can; and 3) Give all you can. The senior elder who assumed the prerogative of evaluating the minister's sermons remarked, 'Those first two points were grand, but the third spoiled it all!' "

After thirty years in the ministry, I likewise have encountered people who have "hangups" when it comes to this matter of giving to God; but I have also discovered that this is nothing new! The Corinthian church experienced the same "hangups," and Paul had to deal with them one by one. This explains why I have concentrated on the Corinthian letters in my expositions of *The Grace of Giving*. In a positive way I have sought to remove the barriers to giving by spelling out the essentiality, the example, the ethics and efficiency of giving. With the appropriate passages before you, I want you to examine carefully the unfolding of Paul's doctrine of *The Grace of Giving;* and then let the Holy Spirit beget the same grace in you.

Thirdly, there is *the blessing of giving*. Of all the feedback I had when preaching these messages, I

---

[2]pp. 33-34

received more letters and comments on what I have called "The Enrichment of Giving," than on any other aspect of our study. Christians have no conception of what they are missing, in terms of enjoyment and enrichment, until they have learned to give on God's terms. After all, the Lord Jesus said: "It is more blessed to give than to receive."[3] The New English Bible renders these words with even more emphasis: "Happiness lies more in giving than in receiving." No wonder these words of the Lord Jesus have been called "The Supreme Beatitude"! And as Tom Rees expressed it, "The only way to prove the truth of this Beatitude is to put it to the test, and we shall soon discover from experience that the word of the Master is true — miserly people are miserable people, and generous people are joyous people."[4]

One other chapter in my book deals with "The Maintenance of the Ministry." Please don't skip it! Preachers rarely speak on this subject lest they be accused of rooting for raises! But quite seriously, this issue of support for the servants of God is so important that it may well determine the continuance or collapse of missionary work abroad and evangelistic endeavor at home. I know of missionaries who have had to be recalled from the field. I also know of colleagues in the ministry who have had to exchange the pulpit or platform for the business office to survive financially. "Brethren, these things ought not to be." God give us grace to take to heart what is meant by "The Maintenance of the Ministry." Only sacrificial giving will make possible the battle for souls in a world that is defiled by sin and beguiled by Satan. And when I speak of sacrificial giving, I mean giving that is measured and motivated by the cross of Christ. It is nothing less than giving at its *best*.

Perhaps a story from the past will illustrate what

---

[3]Acts 20:35
[4]*Money Talks*, p. 9

I mean. During his reign, the king of Prussia, Frederick William III, found himself in great trouble. He was carrying on expensive wars; he was endeavoring to strengthen his country and make a great nation of the Prussian people. But he did not have enough money to accomplish his plans. He could not disappoint his people, and to capitulate to the enemy would be unthinkable.

After careful reflection, he decided to approach the women of Prussia and ask them to bring their jewelry of gold and silver to be melted down and made into money for their country. He resolved, moreover, that for each ornament of gold or silver he would give in exchange a decoration of bronze or iron as a token of his gratitude. Each decoration would bear the inscription, "I gave gold for iron, 1813."

The response was overwhelming. And what was even more important was the fact that these women prized their gifts from the king more highly than their former possessions. The reason, of course, is clear. The decorations were proof that they had sacrificed for their king. Indeed, it is a matter of recorded history that it became unfashionable for women to wear jewelry. So the Order of the Iron Cross was established. Members of this Order wore no ornaments, save a cross of iron for all to see.

What we need in the church today is an army of people who are so committed to the King of kings that sacrifice becomes a way of life! Such an army would do exploits for God; such an army would hasten the coming and reign of the "King eternal, immortal, invisible (and) the only wise God (to whom) be honor and glory for ever and ever."[5]

Recruits for this army should be known as members of The Order of the Cross of Christ because they have experienced *The Grace of Giving*.

---

[5] I Timothy 1:17

THE BASIS OF BLESSING

SCRIPTURE READING

Even from the days of your fathers ye are gone away from mine ordinances, and have not kept them. Return unto me, and I will return unto you, saith the Lord of hosts. But ye said, Wherein shall we return?

Will a man rob God? Yet ye have robbed me. But ye say, Wherein have we robbed thee? In tithes and offerings. Ye are cursed with a curse: for ye have robbed me, even this whole nation.

Bring ye all the tithes into the storehouse, that there may be meat in mine house, and prove me now herewith, saith the Lord of hosts, if I will not open you the windows of heaven, and pour you out a blessing, that there shall not be room enough to receive it.

And I will rebuke the devourer for your sakes, and he shall not destroy the fruits of your ground; neither shall your vine cast her fruit before the time in the field, saith the Lord of hosts. And all nations shall call you blessed: for ye shall be a delightsome land, saith the Lord of hosts.

Your words have been stout against me, saith the Lord. Yet ye say, What have we spoken so much against thee? Ye have said, It is vain to serve God: and what profit is it that we have kept his ordinance, and that we have walked mournfully before the Lord of hosts? And now we call the proud happy; yea, they that work wickedness are set up; yea, they that tempt God are even delivered.

Malachi 3:7-15

1

THE BASIS OF BLESSING

Malachi was the last of the prophets. The times in which he lived, about four hundred years before Christ, are remarkably typical of our day and generation. The religious leaders were failing to proclaim and maintain the laws of God. The house of the Lord was being robbed of its glory, its tithes and offerings. And God's chosen people were intermarrying with the pagan nations around and failing, therefore, to fulfill their rightful responsibilities. So Malachi's message, was one of exposure, rebuke and challenge. Right at the heart of this prophecy, however, this faithful preacher lays down a basis of blessing which applies to all time. In Malachi's day the blessing was primarily material and physical, but in this church age God's purpose for His people is that of spiritual refreshing from the presence of the Lord.

Look, then, at these conditions and observe that if the "windows of heaven" are to be opened unto us in fullness of blessing there must be:

A MORAL RESTORATION

"Even from the days of your fathers ye are gone away from mine ordinances, and have not kept them. Return unto me, and I will return unto you, saith the Lord of hosts." In the philosophy of divine blessing there is no substitute for repentance and obedience. And when nations or individuals depart from the laws of God and manifest a spirit of rebellion heaven demands nothing less than moral restoration. This means *a restoration which is initiated by repentance* — "Return unto me, and I will return unto you, saith the Lord of hosts." Repentance signifies a change of mind leading to a change of heart and life. In essence, it is a "right-about-turn"; a coming back to an offended and grieved God with deep contrition and humility. Let us remember that sin is not only a departure from righteousness, but from God Himself. Therefore, repentance is nothing less than a return to God Himself. And the wonder of it all is that when we return He returns also. "Return unto me," He says, "and I will return unto you." In New Testament language John puts it this way: "If we confess our sins, he is faithful and just to forgive us our sins, and to cleanse us from all unrighteousness."[1] Now, my friend, if you do not know the fullness of blessing in your life, then it is because you have wandered from God. You are in a far-off place, and God is saying to you "Return."

But there is something more than repentance here. There is *a restoration which is perpetuated by obedience* — "Even from the days of your fathers ye are gone away from mine ordinances, and have not kept them." God has shut up blessing to a life of obedience — "This do, and thou shalt live."[2] This is not just a piece of legalism, it is a divine principle of life and blessing. So Malachi solemnly reminds his people that they had departed from God's ordinances, even as their fathers before them. Through Samuel this favored nation had learned and known that "to obey is better than sacrifice, and to hearken than the fat of rams";[3] therefore, there was no excuse.

Tell me, do you want the "windows of heaven" to be opened upon your life? Then fulfill these conditions of repentance and obedience. This is the only way of moral restoration.

---

[1]I John 1:9
[2]Luke 10:28
[3]I Samuel 15:22

Then there is a second condition laid down in our text. It is that of:

A MATERIAL RESTITUTION

"Bring ye all the tithes into the storehouse." The principle of material giving to God is consistent and absolute throughout the Holy Scriptures. When we give, God blesses; and conversely, when we withhold, God curses. So God says, "Ye are cursed with a curse: for ye have robbed me, even this whole nation."

Malachi had to challenge the nation to "bring . . . the tithes" because his people had failed to do this. This is why they were not living in blessing. This word on material restitution is not addressed to givers, but to withholders. And it is important to note *the place of this restitution* — "Bring ye all the tithes into the storehouse." From the time of Hezekiah,[4] there was in the sanctuary a storehouse built for depositing the tithes and offerings of the people. This was also true of the second temple in the days of Nehemiah.[5] But even before this, it was God's clearly prescribed method that all the tithes and offerings of the people were to be brought to *one place*. In fact, if a man lived too far away to carry his corn, wine or firstlings of his herds and flocks, he was instructed to turn his goods into money in order that he might "go unto the place where the Lord his God should choose."[6]

Needless to say, the New Testament counterpart of this principle is the giving of all tithes by the membership to the local church. The disbursements of money may include needs beyond the local church, but the responsibility to bring *all* the tithes and offerings to the local church is plainly illustrated in the Old Testament and definitely taught in the New Testament. One of the great sins of our time is the robbing and de-

---

[4]II Chronicles 31:11
[5]Nehemiah 10:38-39
[6]Deuteronomy 14:22-29

frauding of the local church by its membership. And until such restitution is made, God will not bless. This is what is meant by "storehouse tithing" — the bringing of your tithes and offerings to the place where your membership is established, your spiritual life is nourished, and your church privileges are enjoyed. If you give elsewhere, then it should be over and above the required tithe and offering to your church. Now this is scripturally binding upon all who desire to see the blessing of God.

But notice further *the proportion of this restitution* — "Bring ye all the tithes into the storehouse." It must be pointed out that tithing is four hundred years older than the law. Abraham gave tithes to God through Melchizedek, the king-priest.[7] According to the seventh chapter of Hebrews, Melchizedek is a beautiful type of Christ in resurrection. He gives Abraham bread and wine, symbols of sacrifice, and Abraham acknowledges his indebtedness to God by giving Him tithes of all his spoils. In other words, tithing is the scriptural way of saying "thank You" to God for all that He has done for us.

In his little booklet entitled *Giving to God,* the late Robert A. Laidlaw illustrates this thought by saying: "I go to a home where there is a little girl, five or six years of age, and give her a box of chocolates. She straightway disappears, and when she returns her lips and fingers are covered with chocolate. In another home, however, the box is opened at once, and the little lassie brings it to me and says, 'You have the first one.' 'Oh, no!' I say, 'they are for you.' 'But please,' she pleads, 'you brought them to me, do please have the first one.' And helping myself I say, 'Thank you, dear.' Which child has the warmest place in my affections, and which is more likely to get another box of chocolates?" So the tithe is the first chocolate handed back to God. For some, it will be one-tenth

---

[7]Genesis 14:17—15:1

of the total income (as the word indicates); for others, it will mean more, but never less.

Then there are the offerings. This word means the "free-will giving," which is over and above the basic tithe. The Bible teaches that God *demands* the tithes, whereas He *deserves* our offerings. He demands the tithe because such giving is for our good and blessing. He deserves the offering, for such overflow from our hearts satisfies His heart.

So we see that giving is older than the law,[8] was enforced by the law,[9] was approved by our Lord,[10] and was included in the teaching of the apostles.[11]

Have you been robbing God? Then this is the proportion of restitution which He expects of you if the "windows of heaven" are to be opened upon your life.

Then consider further *the purpose of this restitution* — "Bring ye all the tithes into the storehouse, that *there may be meat in mine house."* The tithes and offerings were the only means by which the priests lived. They had no inheritance of their own.[12] In a similar way, God has ordained that the church should live and function on the human plane by means of the tithes and offerings of His believing people.[13] What is more, the general teaching of the New Testament makes it evident that in normal circumstances each local assembly should be self-supporting.

With this purpose in view, God "curses" those who rob Him. To hold back what is His due in a local church is to merit the judgment of God. This happened in the early history of Israel in Canaan, and it also happened in the early history of the church. Achan's sin was robbing God of the gold of Jericho which was dedicated and designated for the Lord's treasury.[14] The

---

[8]Genesis 14:17—15:1
[9]Leviticus 27:30-33
[10]Matthew 23:23
[11]I Corinthians 16:2
[12]Numbers 18:20-32
[13]I Corinthians 9:1-14
[14]Joshua 6:18-19

penalty was death. What was true of this individual eventually became true of the whole nation in Malachi's day, so that God had to say, "Ye have robbed me." The sin of Ananias and Sapphira was that of robbing God, and the penalty was death.[15] The church age ends with the same problem when the risen Lord has to say to a niggardly Christendom, "Thou art wretched, and miserable, and poor, and blind, and naked."[16]

Faulty stewardship is equivalent to thievery, and God insists that until there is a moral restoration and a material restitution there will be no fullness of blessing. Let us give heed, then, to the place, proportion and purpose of this material restitution.

If such conditions are faithfully met, there is what our text describes as the opened "windows of heaven," or what we might call:

A Miraculous Realization

"Prove me now herewith, saith the Lord of hosts, if I will not open you the windows of heaven." What a concept this is of God's purpose of blessing — "windows of heaven"! This is revival — the outpouring of the Spirit for which we all wait. We cannot work it up, for it is the miraculous realization of God's presence and power. It is the *proving* of God in personal experience. Consider what this blessing includes:

The Rewarding of Our Faith — "I will . . . open you the windows of heaven, and pour you out a blessing, that there shall not be room enough to receive it." What was to be a physical fulfillment of Deuteronomy 11:13-15 in Israel's day is intended to be a spiritual fulfillment in our day. God waits to visit us with "times of refreshing"[17] and floodtides of abundance. The expression, "there shall not be room enough to receive it,"

---

[15]Acts 5
[16]Revelation 3:14-22
[17]Acts 3:19

is difficult to translate from the Hebrew. Literally, it means "until there is sufficiency" which, of course, is understood to signify "until there is no more need." In such a fulfillment faith is not only rewarded, but more than rewarded. Oh, for such a revival!

The Rebuking of Our Foes — "I will rebuke the devourer for your sakes." The locusts had eaten the crops and the mildew and blasting had destroyed what was left. These physical pests and destroying elements represented the enemies of the people of God. Today, they symbolize the forces of Satan that are arrayed against the church. Outside of the experience of revival, there is no authority to rebuke the devil and his hoardes. But once God breaks through from heaven, the enemy is rendered helpless and hopeless. This is what Isaiah means when he says, "When the enemy shall come in like a flood, the Spirit of the Lord shall lift up a standard against him."[18]

The Renewing of Our Fruitfulness — "And all nations shall call you blessed: for ye shall be a delightsome land, saith the Lord of hosts." Malachi is saying here that when the surrounding nations shall see the prosperity which follows upon true giving to God, they will rightly judge that it is the Lord's action in blessing the people.

The world is generally unimpressed by the church's witness today. The average person considers it as irrelevant; the businessman regards it as pathetically inefficient, while the journalist maintains that religious news is little or no news! But what would happen if the sluice gates of heaven were opened and revival blessings poured out upon our local congregations and the church at large? Why the multitudes would throng our buildings, the businessman would take notice, and the reporter would write headlines in our press; in a word, "the nations would call us blessed."

God's purpose for the church is that she should be as

---

[18]Isaiah 59:19

33

"a delightsome land" — a paradise of fruitfulness and fragrance. But since the church is made up of individuals it comes down to you and me. Is the "fruit of the Spirit" evident in your life? Are you living in revival? Is your witness making an impact upon contemporary society? If not, then face seriously and urgently the true basis of blessing:

1) A *moral* restoration. Return to the Lord in repentance and obedience.
2) A *material* restitution. Give God all that you owe Him, in terms of life, tithes and offerings, and according to His promise you will experience
3) A *miraculous* realization. The "windows of heaven" will be opened upon your life.

In a word, pay the price and prove the blessing.

THE ESSENTIALITY OF GIVING

SCRIPTURE READING

Behold, I show you a mystery; We shall not all sleep, but we shall all be changed, in a moment, in the twinkling of an eye, at the last trump: for the trumpet shall sound, and the dead shall be raised incorruptible, and we shall be changed. For this corruptible must put on incorruption, and this mortal must put on immortality. So when this corruptible shall have put on incorruption, and this mortal shall have put on immortality, then shall be brought to pass the saying that is written, Death is swallowed up in victory.

O death, where is thy sting? O grave, where is thy victory? The sting of death is sin; and the strength of sin is the law. But thanks be to God, which giveth us the victory through our Lord Jesus Christ.

Therefore, my beloved brethren, be ye steadfast, unmovable, always abounding in the work of the Lord, forasmuch as ye know that your labor is not in vain in the Lord.

Now concerning the collection for the saints, as I have given order to the churches of Galatia, even so do ye. Upon the first day of the week let every one of you lay by him in store, as God hath prospered him, that there be no gatherings when I come.

And when I come, whomsoever ye shall approve by your letters, them will I send to bring your liberality unto Jerusalem And if it be meet that I go also, they shall go with me.

I Corinthians 15:51—16:4

2

THE ESSENTIALITY OF GIVING

This first epistle to the Corinthians begins with the reminder that "God is faithful, by whom (we are) called unto the fellowship of his Son Jesus Christ our Lord."[1] This theme is then developed with accompanying words of correction and instruction to show that there pulsates throughout the whole church of Christ one common resurrection life by the indwelling presence of the Holy Spirit. The letter finally concludes with the words, "Therefore, my beloved brethren, be ye steadfast, unmovable, always abounding in the work of the Lord, forasmuch as ye know that your labor is not in vain in the Lord. Now concerning the collection for the saints, . . . Upon the first day of the week let every one of you lay by him in store, as God hath prospered him."[2]

In the original there is no break between what we call the fifteenth and sixteenth chapters. So Paul is virtually saying that a *shared* resurrection life in Christ is a *serving* life. In other words, the Lord Jesus gave Himself in death and resurrection, not in order to save us from sacrifice, but rather to teach us how to give ourselves and our substance in continual sacrifice. Thus the apostle finds no difficulty in moving from the theological heights of chapter 15 to the practical depths of chapter 16.

The occasion of this instruction in stewardship was a crisis in the church at Jerusalem. Because of persecution and opposition, many believers had suffered

---

[1] I Corinthians 1:9
[2] I Corinthians 15:58—16:2

the despoiling of their goods and some even the loss of their lives, and Paul felt it was his duty to raise financial assistance for such poverty-stricken saints in the mother church.

Enshrined in this teaching, however, there are principles that will abide for all time. We do well, therefore, to consider this essentiality of giving in three aspects:

THE PURPOSEFUL REGULARITY OF GIVING TO GOD

"Upon the first day of the week let every one of you lay by him in store." One of the outstanding characteristics of our God is that of orderliness and regularity. We see this in nature as well as in the church. The clear word to His believing people is "Let all things be done decently and in order."[3] So in this matter of giving we have definite instruction as to the importance of purposeful regularity.

Observe carefully *the establishment of the holy habit of giving* — "Upon the first day of the week." The history of the church reveals that "the first day of the week" quickly became the day of worship, giving and service for the people of God. Indeed, our text appears to be the earliest mention of this fact. On what better day, therefore, could the Christian take time to settle his accounts with God?

In the Old Testament, the tithe, generally speaking, was an annual tax, but in New Testament times we find that giving to God was to be a weekly contribution. In God's wise economy this was to be the remedy for our weaknesses of indiscipline, irregularity and indifference in our acts of worship. Oh that God would indelibly impress upon us this holy habit of giving upon the *first day of the week!*

Then think of *the encouragement of the high honor of giving* — "Upon the first day of the week let

---

[3] I Corinthians 14:40

every one of you lay by him in store. . . that there be no gatherings when I come." All giving to God should be a matter of theological conviction, leading to practical expression. Too often we have dishonored this holy habit by using carnal pressures to extract money from uninstructed and undisciplined Christians.

The Apostle Paul insists that giving is not only a holy habit but a high honor. This is why he wanted the collections to be made before his arrival in Corinth. He did not want their generosity to depend upon his presence. How far removed is this from the general practice in churches today! With shame we have to confess that so often certain preachers are asked to occupy pulpits because it is known that their presence will insure a good offering. This is unscriptural and certainly unspiritual.

Thus we see that the purposeful regularity of giving to God is bound up with the holy habit and high honor of this ministry. Let us see to it that we never forget this essential principle in the matter of stewardship.

The Personal Responsibility of Giving to God

"Let every one of you lay by him in store." Let us remember that though these words are addressed to the whole church throughout time they also have a particular relevance for the local assembly. Paul was writing to the church of God which was at Corinth.[4] What was true of Corinth could be true of any local congregation in the world today. With this in mind let us note carefully two things:

The Inclusiveness of This Personal Responsibility — "Let *every one of you* lay by him in store." No one in membership is excluded. The words are specific and the application is inescapable. Old and young, rich and poor, must all be involved in this matter of Christian stewardship. Indeed, as Paul reveals later in his sec-

[4] I Corinthians 1:2

ond letter to the Corinthians, the churches of Macedonia gave liberally, and did so out of "deep poverty."[5] Let us never forget that our Lord accepted the widow's mite so that no one could be too poor to give, but He also received the wealth of Barnabas so that no one could be too rich to sacrifice for God!

But this principle of personal responsibility goes even deeper. Money has an inclusiveness about it, because God always associates the gift with the giver; that is to say, giving is essentially personal. Money has no value whatsoever, unless it is the expression of life, labor and love. Furthermore, God has no favorites in His purpose of blessing and since He wants to bless everyone He expects everyone to give. This is why the Lord Jesus said, "It is more blessed to give than to receive."[6]

With this inclusiveness of responsibility, consider further *the directiveness of this personal responsibility* — "Let every one of you *lay by him in store.*" The thought conveyed in the phrase, "lay by him in store," is quite suggestive. In Way's translation it reads "form a little hoard." This, of course, is the proper kind of hoarding. It is something which is deliberately and dedicatively set aside for the Lord Himself. It involves thought, time and planning in this whole matter of stewardship and puts to shame the present-day procedure of so many who come to worship without the preparation or consecration of their gifts. So we see that this laying by in store is an activity of stewardship which takes place before the money is brought to the central treasury of the church. This obviates any hastiness or untidiness in the whole area of giving. Thus it is clear that all giving represents personal responsibility to God. No one is excluded and no one can act without thoughtfulness or deliberateness.

But there is still another aspect which deserves our investigation:

---

[5]II Corinthians 8:2
[6]Acts 20:35

"Lay by . . . as God hath prospered." Reciprocity is the principle of taking and giving; and what Paul is teaching here is that we cannot always be taking without giving. If we have any sense of reasonableness and responsiveness, we are bound to reciprocate in some measure what God so bountifully lavishes upon us. So we have two thoughts emerging: first, *the consideration of what we receive of God* — "Lay by . . . as God hath prospered." We must remember that the prospering of God is never limited to the material gains of our daily work. Spiritually, He blesses us "with all spiritual blessings . . . in Christ";[7] physically, He prospers us with health and strength, "for in him we live, and move, and have our being";[8] temporally, He continually "loads us with benefits."[9] Then over and above this He supplies that by which we live our normal lives: the talents, time and strength for our toil; these are all of His giving. We need to remember this when we face up to our responsibilities of giving to God. Indeed, all giving reflects the measure of our appreciation of God's prospering hand upon us.

But with this consideration of what we receive of God, there is also *the calculation of what we return to God* — "Lay by . . . as God hath prospered." Now before we consider this in terms of our regular giving it might be well to point out that the collection for which Paul was asking was something over and above the normal giving of the church at Corinth. Of the six or more words that are used in the New Testament to describe our monetary gifts to God, the apostle uses a special term in our text which means "an extra collection." The Greek word "logia" denotes that which

[7]Ephesians 1:3
[8]Acts 17:28
[9]Psalm 68:19

was opposite to a tax; in other words, it was *an extra piece of giving*.

With this significant observation, we may now proceed to point out that Paul does not state the exact amount that we are to give to God, but leaves the matter open to the practical reasonableness of every yielded believer. Instructed Christians in the apostle's day would know that under the law the Jew was bound to give one-tenth of his income to God. Then, of course, there were freewill offerings, trespass offerings and costly journeys to the temple. Indeed, it has been estimated that the aggregate of religious gifts among the Jews in olden times could not have been less than one-fifth of each man's income, and some very probably involved one-third of it. This is something seriously to bear in mind when we talk so glibly about *a basic tithe*.

Now the point is, if the Old Testament saints, under law, could give amounts of this kind, can we, under grace, give God any less? So the New Testament leaves this matter wide open for us to act in proportion to the prospering of God. It is important to emphasize, in this connection, that believers owe everything to God, and that yielded believers have given everything to God. Indeed, were this not so, there would be no basis for Christian stewardship. But having made that clear, the Bible goes on to show that, in terms of practical living, while everything may be dedicated to God, our Heavenly Father still demands in cash or kind the basic tithe, and still deserves in cash or kind *the extra offering*. For some, giving will represent more than this, but for no one will it involve less.

So, the final word is summed up in our text: "Let every one of you lay by him in store, as God hath prospered him." If there is a genuine consideration of what we receive of God, there will be a genuine calculation of what we return to Him. Such giving will cost because the cross inspires it, and the church

42

requires it! And this is how heaven has planned it; so we must give to keep the work of God alive!

In his book, *The Royal Route to Heaven,* Dr. Alan Redpath cites this story: "A certain Christian once said to a friend, 'Our church costs too much. They are always asking for money.' Her friend replied in this fashion: 'Some time ago a little boy was born in our home. He cost us a lot of money from the very beginning: he had a big appetite, he needed clothes, medicine, toys and even a puppy. Then he went to school, and that cost a lot more; later he went to college, then he began dating, and that cost a small fortune! But in his senior year at college he died, and since the funeral he hasn't cost us a penny. Now which situation do you think we would rather have?' After a significant pause the friend continued, 'As long as this church lives it will cost. When it dies for want of support it won't cost us anything. A living church has the most vital message for all the world today, therefore I am going to give and pray with everything I have to keep our church alive.' "[10]

So we have considered the essentiality of giving. To take this truth seriously will make great demands upon us; but before we refuse to bow to the Word of God, let us remember that this is the price of keeping our church alive, and she must live if the Savior is to be glorified and the world is to be evangelized. May God give us the grace, then, to be purposeful, personal and practical in our giving, and blessing will most surely come to our lives as well as to our church.

CENTRAL CHURCH OF CHRIST
VULCAN, ALBERTA   TOL 2B0

---

[10]pp. 226-227

THE EXAMPLE OF GIVING

SCRIPTURE READING

Moreover, brethren, we do you to wit of the grace of God bestowed on the churches of Macedonia; how that in a great trial of affliction, the abundance of their joy and their deep poverty abounded unto the riches of their liberality.

For to their power, I bear record, yea, and beyond their power they were willing of themselves; praying us with much entreaty that we would receive the gift, and take upon us the fellowship of the ministering to the saints.

And this they did, not as we hoped, but first gave their own selves to the Lord, and unto us by the will of God. Insomuch that we desired Titus, that as he had begun, so he would also finish in you the same grace also.

Therefore, as ye abound in every thing, in faith, and utterance, and knowledge, and in all diligence, and in your love to us, see that ye abound in this grace also. I speak not by commandment, but by occasion of the forwardness of others, and to prove the sincerity of your love.

For ye know the grace of our Lord Jesus Christ, that, though he was rich, yet for your sakes he became poor, that ye through his poverty might be rich.

II Corinthians 8:1-9

3

THE EXAMPLE OF GIVING

Paul's conception of giving is a lofty one. To him, *giving is a grace*; a ministry of the Holy Spirit inwrought in personal experience, and outworked in practical expression. Wherever he planted churches, the apostle made it his business to instruct the people of God in the doctrine of Christian stewardship. As a consequence, the churches in Macedonia, such as Thessalonica, Berea, and particularly Philippi, were renowned for their charity and liberality.

In the passage now before us, the apostle brings this fact to the attention of the Corinthians and concludes the paragraph with the supreme example of the self-giving of our Lord. Apparently even though this assembly abounded in such gifts as "faith, and utterance, and knowledge, and . . . all diligence," it lacked in the grace of giving. So Paul confronts them with these two examples of giving to beget in them a sense of responsibility in Christian stewardship. Let us then look at the examples and learn the lessons that God would teach us.

THE EXAMPLE OF HUMAN GIVING

"Moreover, brethren, we do you to wit of the grace of God bestowed on the churches of Macedonia." The New English Bible makes this a little clearer by rendering the text as follows: "We must tell you, friends, about the grace of generosity which God has imparted to our congregation in Macedonia." As Paul has indicated already in his first letter to the Corinthians, the occasion of this interchurch money-raising program was the need of Jewish Christians in Jerusalem. Persecution and privation had left the mother church in desperate need of assistance from outside. News of this had reached the believers in Macedonia, and they had risen nobly to the challenge. "Now," says Paul, addressing the Corinthians, "you do like-wise." Then he proceeds to describe in detail the example of this giving on the part of the Macedonians.

It Was Sacrificial Giving — "Moreover, brethren, we make known to you (ASV) the grace of God bestowed on the churches of Macedonia; how that in a great trial of affliction, the abundance of their joy and their deep poverty abounded unto the riches of their liberality." Paul takes great care to show that it was not in circumstances of prosperity that the saints in Macedonia gave their liberal offering. Some severe test of affliction had come upon these local churches[1] and they had been reduced to what is described as "deep poverty" or, more literally, "down-to-the-bottom poverty." But in all their affliction and poverty there was joy and liberality. This is true sacrifice, and they had learned it, as we shall see presently, from their matchless Savior, "who for the joy that was set before him endured the cross, despising the shame."[2]

Dr. Roy L. Laurin tells of a Christian businessman who was traveling in Korea. One day he saw in the field by the side of the road a young man pulling a rude plow, while an old man held the handles. The businessman was amused and took a snapshot of the scene. "That is a curious picture! I suppose these people are very poor," he said to the missionary, who was interpreter and guide to the party. "Yes," was the quiet reply, "those two men happen to be Christians. When their church was being built, they were eager to give something toward it; but they had no money. So they decided to sell their one and only ox and gave the proceeds to the church. This spring they

[1]Acts 16:20; 17:5, 13; Philippians 1:28; I Thessalonians 1:6; 2:14; 3:3-9
[2]Hebrews 12:2

48

are pulling the plow themselves." The businessman was silent for some moments. Then he said, "That must have been a real sacrifice." "They did not call it that," said the missionary, "they rather thought it was fortunate that they had an ox to sell." Needless to say, the businessman was silent. When he reached home, however, he took the picture to his pastor and told him all about it. Then he added, "I want to double my giving to the church, and do some *plow* work. Up until now I have never given God anything that involved real sacrifice."

The Macedonians gave with joy and liberality. It was sacrificial giving. But notice, further, *it was spontaneous giving* — "For to their power, I bear record, yea, and beyond their power they were willing of themselves; praying us with much entreaty that we would receive the gift, and take upon us the fellowship of the ministering to the saints." The Scriptures make it clear that the grace of giving is not so much the result of *outward compulsion* as the consequence of *inward expulsion!* In a very real sense it is "the expulsive power of a new affection." Thus Paul admits that he had no authority to demand offerings from the Corinthian saints, but he could certainly afford them the opportunity to "prove the sincerity of (their) love." And the example he holds up is the giving of these Macedonians who sacrificed even beyond their power. The secret was simple: they "gave of their own free will." This is an accurate rendering of the phrase, "they were willing of themselves." What is more, they took the initiative in beseeching Paul "with much entreaty" that he would receive their gifts as a token of their fellowship with the saints in Jerusalem.

Thus we see that spontaneous giving is not careless giving. Rather, it is giving that is prompted by the Spirit of God and guided by the Word of God. What an example are these dear saints of Macedonia to the church of our day! Would to God that we knew something of sacrifice and spontaneity in our giving!

But there is still another lesson from their example of stewardship: *it was spiritual giving* — "And this they did, not as we hoped, but first gave their own selves to the Lord, and unto us by the will of God." In other words, their giving was the outward expression of their utter dedication to God; or as someone has put it, "The crowning point of their generosity was their complete self-surrender."

There is a kind of giving which is unspiritual; it has ulterior motives. One form of it is drawing attention to one's self. Such a motive the Lord Jesus soundly condemned in His Sermon on the Mount. He said: "When thou doest alms, let not thy left hand know what thy right hand doeth: that thine alms may be in secret."[3] Another form of unspiritual giving is to bring our offerings to God with a spirit of ill-will and reluctance. This, of course, runs contrary to the apostolic injunction to give with purpose of heart — "not grudgingly, or of necessity: for God loveth a cheerful giver."[4] The worst form of giving, however, is that of attempting to buy off one's indebtedness to God.

How different was the spirit of the Macedonians! Not only was their giving unostentatious, joyous and generous, it was accompanied by an act of "complete self-surrender." The construction of the verse before us indicates that the giving of themselves to the Lord and to the apostle was a deeper act of commitment. The word "first" is not used here in a temporal sense but rather with the idea of "the prior claim": "They . . . first gave their own selves to the Lord, and unto us by the will of God." This means that before their generous giving these people had dedicated themselves afresh to the Lord, placed themselves unreservedly in the apostle's hands for the service of Christ, and then provided the monetary support for

[3]Matthew 6:3-4
[4]II Corinthians 9:7

the saints in Jerusalem. This is spiritual giving! **Once** again we exclaim, what an example of human giving is depicted for us in these verses! And if we would ask further to know their secret, surely the answer is that the manner of their giving was the measure of their love for Christ, their Savior and Lord.

It is said that when the British Government sought to reward General Gordon for his brilliant service in China, he declined all money and titles but accepted a gold medal inscribed with the record of his thirty-three engagements. It was his most prized possession. But after his death the medal could not be found. Eventually it was learned that he had sent it to Manchester during a severe famine, directing that it should be melted down and used to buy food for the poor. Under the date of its sending were these words in his diary: "The last earthly thing I had in this world that I valued I have given to the Lord Jesus Christ."

Wonderful as is the example of human giving, Paul does not leave us at this point. He immediately proceeds to describe:

The Example of Divine Giving

"For ye know the grace of our Lord Jesus Christ, that, though he was rich, yet for your sakes he became poor, that ye through his poverty might be rich." In this one all-embracing and matchless sentence, Paul shows that the Holy Spirit who prompted the Macedonians in their giving is the same eternal Spirit who sustained the Savior when He "offered himself without spot to God."[5] In other words, Christ's giving of Himself was sacrificial, spontaneous and spiritual. Consider this a little more closely.

Christ's Giving was Sacrificial — "For ye know the grace of our Lord Jesus Christ, that, though he was rich, yet for your sakes he became poor." The tense of the verb suggests that the fact of the incarnation,

[5]Hebrews 9:14

rather than the conditions under which Jesus lived, was uppermost in Paul's mind. To the apostle, Christ became poor in the very act of becoming man! He just could never get over the condescension and sacrifice of our Lord in contracting to the measure of a woman's womb. So he declares in another place: "And without controversy great is the mystery of godliness: God was manifest in the flesh."[6]

Just think of Him as rich in power, yet humbly submitting to human weakness; rich in glory, yet willingly laying aside that effulgence for the likeness of men; rich in wisdom, yet mysteriously surrendering the independent use of His mind in order to become subject to His Father's judgment; rich in resources, yet having no room at His birth,[7] no home in His life,[8] and no grave at His death.[9]

To Paul, and to those who have sensibilities at all, this is grace; this is unmerited favor; this is unbounded kindness; this is sacrifice in giving at its loftiest and best. Such grace and sacrifice cause us to exclaim:

O matchless grace, that Jesus there alone
On Calvary's cross for sinners did atone:
To such a Friend, our Saviour and our King,
Our lives for service we will gladly bring.

T. L. Hargrave

But notice further that *Christ's giving was spontaneous* — "Though he was rich, yet for your sakes he *became* poor." In perfect harmony with the Father and the Holy Spirit, He took the initiative in coming to earth to give Himself a ransom for you and me. Paul spells out the spontaneity of self-giving when he declares: "The righteousness which is of faith speaketh on this wise, Say not in thine heart, Who shall ascend

---

[6]I Timothy 3:16
[7]Luke 2:7
[8]Matthew 8:20
[9]Matthew 27:59-60

into heaven? (that is, to bring Christ down from above:) or, Who shall descend into the deep? (that is, to bring up Christ again from the dead)."[10] In other words, whether it was the condescending grace of the incarnation, or the conquering grace of the resurrection, it was all of Christ. This is heaven's standard of giving, and there is no substitute for it.

Then note once more that *Christ's giving was spiritual* — "He became poor, that ye through his poverty might be rich." It was entirely selfless and with the supreme object of enriching others. This is spiritual giving.

In the days of the American Revolutionary War there lived at Ephrata, Pennsylvania, a Baptist pastor by the name of Peter Miller who enjoyed the friendship of General Washington. There also dwelt in that town one Michael Wittman, an evil-minded man who did all in his power to abuse and oppose this pastor. One day Michael Wittman was involved in treason and was arrested and sentenced to death. The old preacher started out on foot and walked the whole seventy miles to Philadelphia to plead for this man's life. He was admitted into Washington's presence and at once begged for the life of the traitor. "No, Peter," said Washington, "I cannot grant you the life of your friend." "My friend!" exclaimed the preacher, "he is the bitterest enemy I have." "What?" cried Washington, "you have walked seventy miles to save the life of an enemy? That puts the matter in a different light. I will grant the pardon." And he did. And Peter Miller took Michael Wittman from the very shadow of death, back to his own home in Ephrata — no longer as an enemy, but as a friend.

This is what Jesus did for you and me in His self-giving. He had no other interests than His Father's glory and our salvation and enrichment.

What shall we say then to such teaching? We have

---

[10]Romans 10:6-7

53

seen the highest example of giving in the gracious self-emptying of our Savior; we have observed the same spirit of sacrifice, spontaneity and spirituality in the giving of the Macedonians. Can we do any less? A thousand times no! With all our spiritual blessings and material benefits we are committed to such giving without reserve and without regret. Our song and prayer must ever be:

> When I survey the wondrous cross,
> On which the Prince of glory died,
> My richest gain I count but loss,
> And pour contempt on all my pride.
>
> Were the whole realm of nature mine,
> That were a present far too small;
> Love so amazing, so divine,
> Demands my soul, my life, my all.

Isaac Watts

THE ETHICS OF GIVING

SCRIPTURE READING

And herein I give my advice: for this is expedient for you, who have begun before, not only to do, but also to be forward a year ago.

Now therefore perform the doing of it; that as there was a readiness to will, so there may be a performance also out of that which ye have.

For if there be first a willing mind, it is accepted according to that a man hath, and not according to that he hath not.

For I mean not that other men be eased, and ye burdened: but by an equality, that now at this time your abundance may be a supply for their want, that their abundance also may be a supply for your want; that there may be equality:

As it is written, He that had gathered much had nothing over; and he that had gathered little had no lack.

II Corinthians 8:10-15

4

THE ETHICS OF GIVING

Having warmed the hearts of the Corinthians with the *example* of sacrificial, spontaneous and spiritual giving, as exercised by the Macedonian saints and evidenced by our Lord Jesus Christ, Paul proceeds to deal with the *ethics* of giving. He is well aware of the fact that in no other area of life is corruption more possible than in the handling of money. Recall, for instance, his solemn words to Timothy: "But they that desire to be rich fall into a temptation and a snare and many foolish and hurtful lusts, such as drown men in destruction and perdition. For the love of money is a root of all kinds of evil."[1] This implies that while the *gaining* of money can be a curse to the Christian, so can the *giving* of money; hence the need for the ethics of giving. Before us we have three of comprehensive and vital significance:

THERE IS INTEGRITY IN GIVING

"Herein I give my advice: for this is expedient for you, who have begun before, not only to do, but also to be forward a year ago. Now therefore perform the doing of it; that as there was a readiness to will, so there may be a performance also out of that which ye have." With consummate tact, the apostle proffers his advice to a church that had failed to keep a promise and observe a timetable in their responsibility of giving. Such behavior had manifestly endangered integrity in giving. What a word this is for us today!

---

[1] I Timothy 6:9-10, R.V.

How easy it is for dishonesty and delay to mar and hinder our Christian stewardship!

Paul teaches us that integrity in giving demands *honesty in keeping our trust with God* — "This is expedient for you, who have begun before . . . now to perform the doing of it." Paul was virtually saying that it was morally imperative for their performance to catch up and match up with the vows and pledges that they had made. It appears that the Corinthian church was one of the first to hear of the need in Jerusalem and to offer help. In fact, Paul had used their enthusiastic promise of financial assistance to challenge the churches of Macedonia. He could say: "Your zeal hath provoked very many."[2] Contrary to expectation, however, the Corinthians had failed, while the Macedonians had excelled themselves in liberality out of "deep poverty." The solemn fact was that the Corinthians had not kept their *trust* with God.

It is a serious thing to make a vow and then to break it. Consider what God says about this. "When thou vowest a vow unto God, defer not to pay it; for he hath no pleasure in fools: pay that which thou hast vowed. Better is it that thou shouldest not vow, than that thou shouldest vow and not pay . . . wherefore should God be angry at thy voice, and destroy the work of thine hands?"[3] At the same time, God expects us to make pledges and keep them. A pledge is a trust with God and we must believe God to fulfill it. So many people say that they are afraid to commit themselves in giving, lest they should fail God. But surely that is not only a lack of faith but also a lack of discipline, careful planning and common sense. As someone has pointed out, we live on the principle of pledging every day of our lives. We use electric power on the basis of the pledge to pay for it at the end of the month. We use our telephone on the basis of a pledge. We use every utility we have on the basis of a pledge and think

[2]II Corinthians 9:2
[3]Ecclesiastes 5:4-6

nothing about it. And yet in God's work we say that we dare not risk a pledge. We do not credit God with the wisdom and understanding to make allowances for sicknesses and circumstances beyond our control. We think of Him only as an unbending creditor who will hold us to pledges that we cannot keep. This kind of attitude only reveals the low concept we have of our trust with God. We need to ask the Holy Spirit to teach us integrity in giving.

My heart was greatly encouraged some time ago when this honesty in giving affected an unknown donor within the fellowship of our own church. Whoever it was put an envelope in the collection plate with only one word upon it: "Restitution." In that envelope were six one hundred dollar bills. This was honesty in keeping a trust with God. May God speak similarly to all our hearts.

But integrity in giving also demands *honesty in keeping our time with God* — "And herein I give my advice: for this is expedient for you, who have begun before, not only to do, but also to be forward *a year ago*." Paul tells us here that the Corinthians had pledged their offering for Jerusalem no less than twelve months previously. Quite obviously something had occurred to delay their good intentions. A study of the epistle leaves us in no doubt as to why they had been preoccupied: they had been quarreling and contending over matters which should have been settled at the cross and immediately forgotten.

How true this is in the lives of Christians and churches generally. We pledge ourselves, our substance or our service to God, only to defer our good intentions and break our promises because of carnal preoccupations. The Bible says, "To every thing there is a season, and a time to every purpose under the heaven."[4] And Paul adds, "The time is short";[5]

4Ecclesiastes 3:1
5I Corinthians 7:29

and again, "Redeeming the time, because the days are evil."[6] Has it ever occurred to you that a gift loses its maximum value to God if it is out of timing with the plan of God? To delay until tomorrow what God expects you to do today is to rob your act of giving of its full moral significance.

This brings up the whole question of whether or not we should leave our giving until we have departed this life. Someone has said that those who defer their gifts to their deathbeds virtually say to God: "We will now give You something that we can keep no longer." Happy, therefore, is the man who is his own executor! In this connection have you ever stopped to think of the uncounted millions of dollars in the hands of Christian men and women that are withheld from Christian service until death releases these vast resources? A study of the New Testament definitely questions the wisdom and rightness of this kind of stewardship. That is *not* to say that we are to be irresponsible for our daily expenses, for the Scripture says, "Owe no man any thing."[7] Nor does it mean that we are not to lay up for our dependents, for once again the Word of God declares, "If any provide not for his own, and specially for those of his own house, he hath denied the faith, and is worse than an infidel."[8] But having taken these matters into consideration, it is doubtful whether we shall be rewarded for what happens after we pass off the scene. When the apostle speaks of recompense at the judgment seat of Christ, he clearly states that we are to be reviewed for "the things done in *our bodies*."[9] This means, of course, actions taken while we are still alive and responsible.

So you see that integrity is not only the matter of honesty in keeping our *trust* with God, but also honesty in keeping our *time* with God. These Corin-

---

[6]Ephesians 5:16
[7]Romans 13:8
[8]I Timothy 5:8
[9]II Corinthians 5:10

thians were a year late and Paul was writing to remind them solemnly of this.

But now think with me again of another aspect of our subject:

There Is Ability in Giving

"For if there be first a willing mind, it is accepted according to that a man hath, and not according to that he hath not." The sense of this text leads us to believe that God holds all men and women responsible for their measure of ability to give. Or, to put it in another form, the test of generosity and faithfulness in our stewardship is not our wealth, but rather our willingness to give what we have. That is why Paul emphasizes "if there be first a willing mind, it is accepted according to that a man hath, and not according to that he hath not."

Dr. Roy L. Laurin puts it perfectly when he says: "If you give a dollar, and someone gives one hundred dollars, the smallness of your gift would not be measured by the largeness of the other person's gift; the measurement would be according to what you have and the willingness with which you gave what you had."

To analyze this principle a little more closely, let us consider it as follows. There is *an intent in the ability of giving* — "For if there be first a willing mind, it is accepted." This matter of intent cannot be overemphasized. There are many people who give merely to maintain their reputation, or to silence the voice of conscience; but what pleases God is the spontaneous intention of a willing mind, and that is why the Hebrew writer says, "To do good and to communicate forget not: for with such sacrifice God is well pleased."[10] If the clear intention to give is already in the heart, the amount is of secondary importance. What constitutes the sacrifice which pleases the heart of God is

[10]Hebrews 13:16

61

the willingness of mind to give in response to the greatest Gift of all, even the Lord Jesus Christ.

This aspect of truth is beautifully demonstrated by David in his desire to build a temple.[11] His love to God was so great that he wished to express it in the form of a sanctuary in which the law of God could be read, and the will of God revealed. But you will remember that when he bared his heart to Jehovah he was told, "Thou hast shed blood abundantly, and hast made great wars: thou shalt not build a house unto my name, because thou hast shed much blood upon the earth in my sight."[12] So David was left with the privilege of preparing the materials while his son Solomon erected the temple. The point of the story, however, is that the intention to build a temple was in the heart of only one man — and that was David. We need a willingness of mind, both in regard to our responsibility and our privilege in giving.

But with this intent in the ability of giving there is also *an extent in the ability of giving.* Paul says that giving is "accepted according to that a man hath, and not according to that he hath not." What is your attitude toward your stewardship responsibilities? Someone has said that responsibility, for Christians, is "our response to God's ability." And then he adds: "There are five possible attitudes: 1) We may *shirk* our responsibilities; 2) We may *shelve* them, hoping that at some time or other we may fulfill them; 3) We may *shoulder* them, and wear ourselves out bearing their full weight; 4) We may *shed* them after having made an attempt to fulfill them; or 5) We may *share* them. It is following the fifth course that we shall be best able to fulfill the law of Christ and bring glory to God."

In summing up the ethics involved in the ability to give we do well to recall the story of Ananias and

[11] II Samuel 7
[12] I Chronicles 22:8

Sapphira.[13] Here we see the two aspects of intent and extent in giving solemnly illustrated. Peter made it very plain, in addressing Ananias, that while their joint estate remained, it was their own, and after it was sold it was in their own power or ability to give as God should guide them; that is to say, God's purpose is never to press us to give what we cannot, but only that which we are able. The failure, however, in the case of these two was in their intent. They agreed to give part of the price in the name of the whole, and for this unethical procedure they were judged with the stroke of death.

Let us see to it that in all our stewardship we are absolutely ethical in both the intent and extent of ability in giving.

Once again in this passage:

THERE IS EQUALITY IN GIVING

"For I mean not that other men be eased, and ye burdened: but by an equality . . . your abundance may be a supply for their want, that their abundance also may be a supply for your want . . . as it is written, He that had gathered much had nothing over; and he that had gathered little had no lack." The Bible teaches that no believer has a right to enjoy this world's goods while his brother is in need. This explains why the church functioned as it did in those early days of persecution and privation. You will remember that after Pentecost, because of distress and need, "all that believed . . . had all things common; and sold their possessions and goods, and parted them to all men, as every man had need."[14] As we shall see in a moment, such teaching does not in any way support either the Marxist idea of communism or the kind of giving which encourages luxury or laziness.

What is being taught is simply that *in prosperity*

13Acts 5
14Acts 2:44-45

63

we are to relieve the needs of others — "By an equality . . . your abundance may be a supply for their want." John teaches exactly the same principle when he says with searching penetration: "Whoso hath this world's good, and seeth his brother have need, and shutteth up his bowels of compassion from him, how dwelleth the love of God in him?"[15] This concept of equality, of course, applies not only to people in need, but to situations that require financial assistance.

In our day and generation the great proportion of giving in our churches is directed to such causes as missions, radio, television, social services and other ministries for reaching and helping the lost. While we are *able* to support such endeavors we are *committed* so to do. This, we repeat, is equality in giving. Paul warns, however, that equality in giving should not cause the saints in Jerusalem to be eased, while others are burdened. In other words, "the Jerusalem saints were not to enjoy plush seats while the Corinthian Christians sat on hard benches!" On the contrary, there should be wisdom and a sense of balance in this whole matter of sharing the resources of a local church.

Then Paul takes pains to show that the reverse is just as true: *in adversity we are to receive the gifts of others* — "Their abundance also may be a supply for *your* want; that there may be equality." Now there are some people who will not accept gifts lest they should be obligated to the donors. This, in Paul's view, is unethical. We should receive all that God gives us through our brethren with a holy sense of gratefulness and indebtedness, since the time may well come when we have to reciprocate the kindness shown us. This truth was not for Corinth only; it is relevant today. The fortunes of life change very quickly. Today we may be in abundance while tomorrow we may be in want. Today we may live in luxury while tomorrow we may be experiencing lack. Today we may have the privilege of giving while to-

---

[15]I John 3:17

morrow we may have the equal privilege of receiving. So equality in giving teaches that the rich are not to be expected to bear all the load, and the poor are not to be excused from proportionate responsibility.

To illustrate his point, the apostle cites an incident in Israel's history.[16] It was the case of an Israelite who went out to gather manna. The person who, overcome with greed, appropriated more than was his portion found that the residue turned into a foul mass of pollution. On the other hand, the individual who gathered less than was his due had no lack.

So God levels all His people to the point of equal rights in His presence. If we fail to give in prosperity God will curse what we hold back. And in the same way, if we fail to receive in adversity God will judge us for the pride that hinders us from recognizing His providing hand.

So we have seen the challenging, but clear, teaching on the ethics of giving. The more we study this passage, the more it will become evident that Paul has covered the whole ground of *morality* in the matter of money. To lay these principles to heart is to please God and to live in blessing; to reject them is to break the heart of God and to fall into a "temptation and a snare," which may lead to "destruction and perdition." God expects integrity, ability and equality in our giving, and when we have fulfilled His will let us not imagine that we have done God a favor, but rather followed that which is right; and that in all these things God is no man's debtor. Thus it is written: "For God is not unrighteous to forget your work and labor of love, which ye have showed toward his name, in that ye have ministered to the saints, and do minister."[17]

The story is told of a farmer who was known for his generous giving, and whose friends could not understand how he could give so much away and yet

16Exodus 16:18
17Hebrews 6:10

remain so prosperous. One day a spokesman for his friend said, "We cannot understand you. You give far more than the rest of us and yet you always seem to have more to give." "Oh, that is easy to explain," the farmer said, "I keep shoveling into God's bin and God keeps shoveling into mine, but God has the bigger shovel!" Here was a man whose ethics of giving were controlled by the power of an indwelling Lord.

Tell me, who holds your purse? Is it self, or is your testimony something like this?

> I'm feeling very rich today,
> For Jesus holds my purse.
> I need not count its scanty store
> As all the assets at my door;
> Behind it stands a wealthy name,
> And vast resources I may claim —
> Since Jesus holds my purse.
>
> My Cashier never lets me want —
> Since He controls my purse
> Debit and credit always meet,
> I marvel at His counsel sweet,
> Concerning purchases I make,
> Or money given for His dear sake —
> While He controls my purse.
>
> I'd face the world in great alarm
> If Judas held my purse;
> He'd call the gifts of humble love
> Naught but a waste, treasure above,
> Uncertain quantity and poor.
> My life would barren be, I'm sure,
> If Judas held my purse.
>
> And thus I live a carefree life —
> For Jesus holds my purse.
> Since money is a sacred thing,
> Both joy and sorrow it may bring;
> According as we do His will,
> Or find our hearts rebellious still —
> Let Jesus hold your purse.

Selected

THE EFFICIENCY OF GIVING

SCRIPTURE READING

But thanks be to God, which put the same earnest care into the heart of Titus for you. For indeed he accepted the exhortation; but being more forward, of his own accord he went unto you.

And we have sent with him the brother, whose praise is in the gospel throughout all the churches; and not that only, but who was also chosen of the churches to travel with us with this grace, which is administered by us to the glory of the same Lord, and declaration of your ready mind: avoiding this, that no man should blame us in this abundance which is administered by us: providing for honest things, not only in the sight of the Lord, but also in the sight of men.

And we have sent with them our brother, whom we have oftentimes proved diligent in many things, but now much more diligent, upon the great confidence which I have in you.

Whether any do inquire of Titus, he is my partner and fellow-helper concerning you: or our brethren be inquired of, they are the messengers of the churches, and the glory of Christ. Wherefore show ye to them, and before the churches, the proof of your love, and of our boasting on your behalf.

For as touching the ministering to the saints, it is superfluous for me to write to you: for I know the forwardness of your mind, for which I boast of you to them of Macedonia, that Achaia was ready a year ago; and your zeal hath provoked very many.

Yet have I sent the brethren, lest our boasting of you should be in vain in this behalf; that, as I said, ye may be ready: lest haply if they of Macedonia come with me, and find you unprepared, we (that we say not, ye) should be ashamed in this same confident boasting.

Therefore I thought it necessary to exhort the brethren, that they would go before unto you, and make up beforehand your bounty, whereof ye had notice before, that the same might be ready, as a matter of bounty, and not as of covetousness.

II Corinthians 8:16—9:5

5

THE EFFICIENCY OF GIVING

In our last study we were thinking of the ethics of giving. Paul both announces and applies these principles with solemn authority. But now in the process of logical development he deals with a matter which calls for equal consideration and implementation in the local church: it is the question of the efficiency of giving. In effect, the apostle is saying that there is no point in exhorting God's people to give generously and ethically if the management of such stewardship is lacking in efficiency. Church members, and particularly officers, are responsible to God and to men for honesty in the handling of money, and equal wisdom in the using of it. So the verses before us deal with two main considerations:

THE MOTIVATION OF EFFICIENT GIVING

"Providing for honest things, not only in the sight of the Lord, but also in the sight of men." With these words Paul confronts his readers with a twofold motivation which should determine not only Christian giving, but also Christian living. The first is *the glory of God*. He makes this manifestly clear when he says: "This grace, which is administered by us to the glory of the . . . Lord." Already he has touched upon this motivation in his first letter to the Corinthians where he says, "Whatsoever ye do, do all to the glory of God."[1] Anything less than fulfilling the will of God to the glory of God is defined in Holy Scripture as sin: "For all

---

[1] I Corinthians 10:31

69

have sinned, and come short of the glory of God."[2]

What is more, the Catechism makes it clear that "man's chief end is to glorify God and to enjoy Him forever." Therefore we are to glorify God by our worshipful praise: "Whoso offereth praise glorifieth me."[3] We are to glorify Him by our consistent fruitbearing: "Herein is my Father glorified, that ye bear much fruit."[4] We are to glorify Him by our spiritual unity: "That ye may with one mind and one mouth glorify God, even the Father of our Lord Jesus Christ."[5] We are to glorify Him by our entire dedication: "For ye are bought with a price: therefore glorify God in your body, and in your spirit, which are God's."[6] And last, but not least, we are to glorify Him by our good works: "Let your light so shine before men, that they may see your good works, and glorify your Father which is in heaven."[7] In this last category is included this matter of giving. Only in this way shall we provide for "honest things . . . in the sight of the Lord." The glory of God, then, should ever motivate us to give and to give our best.

The story is told of an occasion when Queen Mary was walking in the vicinity of Balmoral, Scotland on a dark and cloudy day. She strolled rather far, and as the rain came down she stopped at a cottage for the loan of an umbrella. The woman did not recognize the queen, so decided to give the stranger an old umbrella with a broken rib. The next morning a man in gold braid appeared at the cottage door. "The Queen asked me to thank you for lending her the umbrella," he explained. The woman in the cottage was dumbfounded, and with tears flowing down

---

[2]Romans 3:23
[3]Psalm 50:23
[4]John 15:8
[5]Romans 15:6
[6]I Corinthians 6:20
[7]Matthew 5:16

her cheeks said, "What an opportunity I missed! Why did I not give the Queen the best umbrella I had?"

So let your motivation of efficient giving be the best for God.

The other aspect of this motivation is *the good of man* — "Providing for honest things, not only in the sight of the Lord, *but also in the sight of men."* Paul amplifies and explains this in the previous verse where he says: "Avoiding this, that no man should blame us in this abundance which is administered by us." Paul recognized how important it was that the contributions of the churches, both in Macedonia and Corinth, for the poor saints in Jerusalem, should be handled with scrupulous care so that neither he nor his associates would be liable to the slightest suspicion of misappropriating other people's money.

What an example the apostle has left us, not only for his day but for the churches of our time! It is so easy for Christian people to suppose that as long as they have an unclouded conscience regarding their acts before God it does not really matter whether they appear honest before their fellow men. Thus the temptation comes in every fellowship of God's people to minimize the importance of making it transparently clear before others that all church actions are beyond suspicion. As one great theologian has said: "It is a foolish pride which leads to a disregard of public opinion." Both Old and New Testaments corroborate this vital principle. Solomon says, "A false balance is abomination to the Lord: but a just weight is his delight."[8] And the Apostle Paul adds, "Provide things honest in the sight of all men."[9]

Thus we see that the efficiency of giving must ever be governed by this twofold motivation — the glory of God and the good of man.

Dr. G. Campbell Morgan recalls that when the Salvation Army started its work General William Booth

[8]Proverbs 11:1
[9]Romans 12:17

was charged with dishonesty. People said that all the property was in his name and that he at any time might have converted that property into money and appropriated it for himself. That was the criticism of the work. However, from the very first, he was careful to publish his accounts, and in the process of the years that criticism ceased entirely.

The same thing happened in the ministry of Dr. Billy Graham. Both in this country and overseas he was accused of conducting his crusades for personal gain; but wisely and scripturally he saw to it that reputable accountants in each city made public all facts and figures relating to a crusade. Furthermore, he insisted on putting himself on salary, in common with the other members of his team. Since those days less and less criticism has been leveled at this evangelist, whom God has so greatly used.

Many other instances could be cited to illustrate this basic principle of the church of "providing for honest things, not only in the sight of the Lord, but also in the sight of men."

But our second consideration has to do with:

The Ministration of Efficient Giving

"Avoiding this, that no man should blame us in this abundance which is administered by us." No one in the Corinthian church could ever accuse Paul of being impracticable or inefficient. Throughout these two epistles he was forever relating the highest concepts of theology to the business of everyday living. This is particularly true of the verses we are now studying. He has just dealt with the solemn theme of the ethics of giving. Now he proceeds to discuss the efficiency of giving. In a word, he says that the motivation of giving must be linked with the ministration of giving; and in the apostle's view this involves *the engagement of efficient men* — "But thanks be to God, which put the same earnest care into the heart of Titus for you

. . . and we have sent with him the brother, whose praise is in the gospel throughout all the churches." And again: "We have sent with them our brother, whom we have oftentimes proved diligent in many things." No one can study these verses without being deeply impressed by the care with which Paul handled this matter of the engagement of efficient men. Titus was obviously his own choice and, as we shall see a little later, his "partner and fellow helper." The other two unnamed brethren were the appointees of the churches involved in the giving. Let us take a few moments to look at them.

Titus, though not mentioned in the Acts, was one of Paul's very close companions and a man in whom he had put a considerable amount of trust. As we have observed, he refers to him as "my partner and fellow helper." Titus had already been to Corinth and, in fact, had been responsible for the delicate task of smoothing over the tense situation which had arisen between Paul and the Corinthians. He was, therefore, a man of great tact and force of character. But what is even more important to note in this context is that he was a leader who possessed great ability as an administrator. Although his primary ministry in the church at Corinth was a spiritual one, it is clear from the reading of chapters 8 and 9 of Second Corinthians that he was also responsible for organizing the money raising program. So Paul asked him to return, accompanied by this very letter, to complete the task of collecting the necessary financial assistance for the saints in Jerusalem.

The second brother mentioned is unnamed, though many believe he may have been Barnabas, John Mark, Luke, or even Apollos! What is said about him, however, is very beautiful and commendable. He was evidently well-known to the Corinthians for his praise-worthy evangelistic ministry throughout all the churches. Consider what Paul says about him: "And we have sent . . . the brother, whose praise is in the gospel throughout all the churches." Here was a man who obviously had a redemptive passion for the lost. One can visualize his children in the faith, not only in the congregations across Macedonia, but also in the church at Corinth.

The third brother referred to is also unnamed, but once again he has a high commendation, for the apostle declares, "We have oftentimes proved (him to be) diligent in many things." W. C. G. Proctor, in his commentary on Second Corinthians, says: "If we allow ourselves a little liberty, we may think of this brother as a Christian accountant . . . who allied his accountancy with evangelism." Apparently the idea behind his diligence suggests the thought that he was particularly capable and reliable in matters financial.

Now let us summarize this information concerning these three men. In Titus we have a pastoral administrator. In the first unnamed brother we have a praiseworthy evangelist, and in the second unnamed man we have a proficient accountant. But what is supremely important is that in all three we have *men of God.* Surely we have to give the apostle unqualified credit for his discernment in the choice of these men. No wonder he could conclude his commendation of his brethren with the glorious words, "They are the messengers of the churches, and the glory of Christ. Wherefore show ye to them, and before the churches, the proof of your love, and of our boasting on your behalf."

Thoughtful people cannot but agree that here is the ministration of efficient giving at its best. This is management at its loftiest. How such teaching shows up the sloppy and slovenly way in which money matters are handled in many of our modern churches! The usual democratic procedure of accepting anyone, so long as he is elected by the church, certainly does not tally with this apostolic standard. Let us point out again that these were men of manifest spirituality, maturity and recognized ability.

Before we leave this point, it is necessary to observe that for this vital task of administering the large sums of money which had been collected, Paul insisted on having at least *three* outstanding men. In this he was following a scriptural principle which is found in both Old and New Testaments, but which Paul particularly emphasizes in the closing paragraphs of the epistle we are studying. The words in question are, "In the mouth of two or three witnesses shall every word be established."[10] So we see the utter importance of engaging efficient men for the high and holy task of stewardship in the life of the church.

With the engagement of efficient men, the apostle is careful also about *the employment of efficient methods*. Already he has said, "Herein I give my advice."[11] Now he adds, "For as touching the ministering to the saints, it is superfluous for me to write to you";[12] and again: "Yet have I sent the brethren."[13] Now if we think through these three statements it will quickly become apparent that the apostle's method of raising money, both for local and general needs, is clearly delineated. There was, first, the *scriptural indoctrination*. When Paul speaks of giving advice, he is not offering his own opinion; he is pressing his exhortation on the basis of sound biblical principles already laid down. Perhaps the essence of his teaching is best summed up in a verse that we have previously considered: "Upon the first day of the week let every one of you lay by him in store, as God hath prospered him, that there be no gatherings when I come."[14] What Paul has said here and elsewhere is that giving to God should be more than an emotional exercise: it should be the consequence of theological conviction; in other

[10]II Corinthians 13:1
[11]II Corinthians 8:10
[12]II Corinthians 9:1
[13]II Corinthians 9:3
[14]I Corinthians 16:2

words, the very opposite of psychological tricks and carnal pressures.

The second aspect of his method was that of *pastoral communication*. He had written once "concerning the collection"[15] and now he communicates with them again. In fact, the two chapters that we are presently considering are the fullest treatment on the grace of giving that we have in the New Testament. Most of what is written, however, is in the form of a pastoral exhortation and is, therefore, a guide to all whose task it is to stir up God's people to fulfill their stewardship responsibilities. So whether by letter or personal exhortation, the pastor of a church has an apostolic precedent to follow in challenging Christians to give. We are certainly to trust God to meet our needs, but we are also to inform His people and to provide them with an opportunity "to prove the sincerity of (their) love."[16]

The last aspect of the apostolic method was that of *official administration*. He says, "Yet have I sent the brethren."[17] We have already examined these men and their eminent suitability for the task to which they were committed; but what I want you to observe is that they had an official mandate to administer the offerings. These chosen men were to assume that because of scriptural teaching and pastoral exhortation they were free to collect the gifts from the church treasury, determine a reckoning of them, and then prepare them for transportation to Jerusalem. In effect, their task was to see that individual members, as well as the church corporate, were following through on their stewardship responsibilities. Thank God for every local church that has a Board of Deacons "of honest report, full of the Holy Ghost and wisdom,"[18] who are able not only to challenge the membership con-

---

[15] I Corinthians 16:1
[16] II Corinthians 8:8
[17] II Corinthians 9:3
[18] Acts 6:3; I Timothy 3:8-13

cerning these matters, but to give adequate advice on Christian stewardship. It is a sad church, not to say an impossible task, when the responsibility is left entirely to the pastor.

So we have seen that in money matters, as in all other aspects of church life, we are expected to do "all things . . . decently and in order."[19] Let us then ever bear in mind the true motivation of efficient giving and then be careful to follow through on the ministration of efficient giving. Only thus shall we glorify God and edify the church.

At the heart of efficiency is faithfulness, and it costs to be faithful. As someone has pointed out, "It cost Abraham the yielding up of his only son; it cost Esther the risk of her life; it cost Daniel being cast into the den of lions; it cost Shadrach, Meshach and Abednego being put into a fiery furnace; it cost Stephen death by stoning; it cost Peter a martyr's death; it cost Paul his life. Does it cost you anything to be faithful to your Lord and King?" Remember that efficiency is faithfulness in action. Are you prepared to be "faithful unto death"?[20]

[19]I Corinthians 14:40
[20]Revelation 2:10

THE ENRICHMENT OF GIVING

SCRIPTURE READING

But this I say, He which soweth sparingly shall reap also sparingly; and he which soweth bountifully shall reap also bountifully.

Every man according as he purposeth in his heart, so let him give; not grudgingly, or of necessity: for God loveth a cheerful giver.

And God is able to make all grace abound toward you; that ye, always having all sufficiency in all things, may abound to every good work: (as it is written, He hath dispersed abroad; he hath given to the poor: his righteousness remaineth for ever.

Now he that ministereth seed to the sower both minister bread for your food, and multiply your seed sown, and increase the fruits of your righteousness;) being enriched in every thing to all bountifulness, which causeth through us thanksgiving to God.

For the administration of this service not only supplieth the want of the saints, but is abundant also by many thanksgivings unto God; while by the experiment of this ministration they glorify God for your professed subjection unto the gospel of Christ, and for your liberal distribution unto them, and unto all men; and by their prayer for you, which long after you for the exceeding grace of God in you.

Thanks be unto God for his unspeakable gift.

II Corinthians 9:6-15

6

THE ENRICHMENT OF GIVING

In this final paragraph of Second Corinthians 9, Paul climaxes his treatment of the grace of giving with some weighty words on the enriching ministry of Christian stewardship. He is determined not to leave his readers until he has impressed upon them the all-important fact that the grace of giving is God's supreme method of enriching those who dispense gifts as well as those who receive gifts. So he speaks in these verses of four important matters:

THE ENRICHMENT OF FRUITFULNESS IN GIVING

"But this I say, He which soweth sparingly shall reap also sparingly; and he which soweth bountifully shall reap also bountifully." There are laws of harvest that operate not only in the natural, but also in the spiritual realm. Paul is illustrating this fact by drawing attention to the farmer who sows his spring crop. This man knows that what he has sown in the spring he will harvest in the fall. It is just one of those unalterable laws that he will reap what he has sown. Moreover, the farmer is cognizant of the fact that the proportion of his reaping will be determined by the proportion of his sowing. If he is foolish enough to sow sparingly he will reap sparingly; on the other hand, if he is wise enough to sow bountifully he will also reap bountifully. This is a profound principle in all areas of Christian experience, and especially in the area of giving. The believer is to understand that giving is not a question of scattering, but of sowing. It is

81

not a contribution; it is an investment. Thus all giving constitutes a challenge to our faith. No farmer sows without exercising simple faith in the law of harvest. Indeed, if he had no faith he would not sow at all. In his letter to the Galatians Paul speaks specifically of this enrichment of fruitfulness in giving: "Be not deceived; God is not mocked: for whatsoever a man soweth, that shall he also reap. For he that soweth to his flesh shall of the flesh reap corruption; but he that soweth to the Spirit shall of the Spirit reap life everlasting. And let us not be weary in well doing: for in due season we shall reap, if we faint not."[1]

In this passage, which is *primarily* associated with the subject of giving, the apostle points out that there are two kinds of sowing and also two kinds of reaping. *There is a sowing which reaps a carnal harvest* — "He that soweth to his flesh shall of the flesh reap corruption."[2] There is no enrichment in this kind of giving. A carnal Christian sows to his flesh by spending his resources to gratify his own personal desires. Such a person must expect nothing less than the reaping of corruption. In other words, that which might have been rewarded by being invested in the Lord's work will be nothing but "wood, hay and stubble" at the judgment seat of Christ."[3] Careful thought will reveal that this matter of carnal giving impinges upon motives as well as means; for it is not only *what* we give but *how* we give and *why* we give that matters in the presence of God.

Having dealt with the negative aspect, the apostle then indicates that *there is a sowing which reaps a spiritual harvest* — "He that soweth to the Spirit shall of the Spirit reap life everlasting."[4] Here is the enrichment of fruitfulness in giving which is possible for all who will venture out in faith in the ministry of

---

[1]Galatians 6:7-9
[2]Galatians 6:8
[3]I Corinthians 3:12-15
[4]Galatians 6:8

Christian stewardship. The text actually means that as we respond to the indwelling Spirit in love, sacrifice and stewardship, we shall be adding interest to the capital of eternal life which we already have in Christ. Nobody can merit the gift of eternal life by personal works of righteousness, "for by grace are ye saved through faith; and that not of yourselves: it is the gift of God: not of works, lest any man should boast."[5]

But having made that clear, there is a whole body of Scripture which reveals that we can add to our spiritual capital by a continuing enrichment through the ministry of giving. In fact, there is no area of Christian experience which deepens the capacity for more of the gifts of God than that of sacrificial giving. Introduce me to a niggardly Christian and I will show you a person whose Christian life is shriveled up. On the other hand, lead me to a believer who knows the joy of sacrificial giving and I will point out a person whose life is one of fruitful enrichment. I am convinced that one of the reasons why the devil has caused the subject of giving to stir up resistance and resentment among God's people is that he knows there are few ways of spiritual enrichment like the exercise of faithful stewardship. Let us never forget that at the very heart of the Gospel is the whole principle of giving. Heaven could never be enriched with the company of the redeemed if Jesus had not given Himself, even to the death of the cross. And by the same token, we can never enrich the church or our personal lives without sacrificial stewardship. There is no fruitfulness without the ministry of giving.

But let us proceed to observe the second principle which Paul lays down in this passage.

The Enrichment of Joyfulness in Giving

"Every man according as he purposeth in his heart, so let him give; not grudgingly, or of necessity: for

---

[5]Ephesians 2:8-9

God loveth a cheerful giver." Giving not only develops a capacity for fruitfulness but also for joyfulness. Miserableness is always linked with miserliness, whereas merriment is indissolubly associated with magnanimity. To know such joyfulness, however, Paul says that giving must be exercised *without casualness* — "Every man according as he purposeth in his heart, so let him give." This takes us back to principles we have already considered in the earlier chapters. God has given careful instruction as to how we should develop holy habits of "laying by in store."[6] as we have been prospered; and so give out of a true sense of purposefulness and planning. Casualness implies carelessness and heartlessness and, therefore, joylessness. The very discipline which determines a sense of purposefulness is the discipline which deepens joyfulness in our Christian experience. So we are to give without casualness.

Furthermore, we are to give *without complaint* — "So let him give; *not grudgingly.*" This is truly a searching word to all our hearts. Who among us has not to confess that when the challenge of stewardship has come to us, there has risen up within us a spirit of unwillingness and even rebellion? There is no joy in this, and therefore no enrichment. God enable us to bring the unwillingness to give (what God demands and deserves) to the cross, until the joy of giving is born in our souls.

Notice once again in our text that we are to give *without compulsion* — "There should be no reluctance, no sense of compulsion; God loves a cheerful giver" (NEB). The believer must not have as his main motive the consideration of what others will think of him if he refrains from giving. Sad to say, but nonetheless true, a high percentage of giving is motivated by the safeguarding of our good name; but such unworthy thoughts rob Christian stewardship of its love-

---

[6]I Corinthians 16:2

liness and joy. God's purpose is rather that we should experience the enrichment of joyfulness in giving, and so He says, "Every man according as he purposeth in his heart, so let him give; not grudgingly, or of necessity: for God loveth a cheerful giver." As we have been reminded so often, the word "cheerful" here can be rendered "hilarious," suggesting a spirit of real enjoyment which sweeps away all human restraints. The Lord Jesus summed up this enrichment of joyfulness in giving when He said, "It is more blessed to give than to receive."[7] Interesting enough, this astonishing statement is not found in the gospels, and yet Paul uses it in his address to the elders at Ephesus to press home the enrichment which comes through the sacrifice of giving. He says, in effect, that if only these brethren would learn the deep principle of *joy through giving* their lives would be truly blessed. In every local church of Jesus Christ there are people who would rise to testify to the outworking of this spiritual law in their lives. They never knew what it was to be joyful until they learned how to give without casualness, complaint or compulsion.

There is a lovely story told of the saintly Frances Ridley Havergal who wrote the lines we so often sing without due seriousness and commitment:

> Take my silver and my gold,
> Not a mite would I withhold.

It is on record that this hymn was both autobiographical and actual. Frances Ridley Havergal *did* what she sang. In her writings is this personal testimony: " 'Take my silver and my gold' now means shipping off all my ornaments — including a jewel cabinet which is really fit for a countess — to the Church Missionary Society. . . . I don't think I need tell you I never packed a box with such pleasure." This was giving with hilarity!

---

[7] Acts 20:35

85

But now let us move on to the next thought in the apostle's development:

THE ENRICHMENT OF USEFULNESS
IN GIVING

"And God is able to make all grace abound toward you; that ye, always having all sufficiency in all things, may abound to every good work . . . now he that ministereth seed to the sower both minister bread for your food, and multiply your seed sown, and increase the fruits of your righteousness." The *miracle* of giving is that it produces a *ministry* of giving. In other words, when God can trust His people with money, He sees to it that they always have plenty for themselves and more for others. So the apostle quotes Psalm 112:9 to support this divine principle: "He hath dispersed, he hath given to the poor; his righteousness endureth for ever."

Simply stated, this law of enrichment of usefulness in giving works as follows. As we give to God *He meets our requirements* — "Now he that ministereth seed to the sower both minister bread for your food." The God of Elijah is still the same today. When the prophet put himself at God's total disposal he never lacked anything, even though the land was scourged with famine. And even when the brook Cherith dried up and the ravens ceased to bring his daily meal God provided his daily bread.[8] Later David could testify: "I have been young, and now am old; yet have I not seen the righteous forsaken, nor his seed begging bread."[9] In the days of our Lord's earthly sojourn, He could challenge His disciples with the words, "When I sent you without purse, and scrip, and shoes, lacked ye any thing? And they said, Nothing."[10] Then the Apostle Paul sums it up when he

---

[8]I Kings 17
[9]Psalm 37:25
[10]Luke 22:35

says, "I have learned, in whatsoever state I am, therewith to be content. I know both how to be abased, and I know how to abound: every where and in all things I am instructed both to be full and to be hungry, both to abound and to suffer need";[11] and again: "My God shall supply all your need."[12]

So we see that God commits Himself to meet our requirements. But more than this, *He multiplies our resources* — "Now he that ministereth seed to the sower both minister bread for your food, and multiply your seed sown." It is obvious from this verse that God *alone* is responsible for the measure in which these resources are multiplied, for the promise is clear and sure: He multiplies the seed that is sown. So we can safely say that giving is not self-impoverishment but self-enrichment. Indeed, the Lord Jesus affirms that giving is an assurance of gaining. He says, "Give, and it shall be given unto you; good measure, pressed down, and shaken together, and running over, shall men give into your bosom. For with the same measure that ye mete withal it shall be measured to you again."[13] This, of course, must not be our motive for giving "lest we vitiate the whole ethical value of the act. But our Lord offers this assurance, that giving is never a one-way street: it is the door to plenty."

Scores of examples could be cited at this point to illustrate how God multiplies the resources of those who give in the right measure and with the right motive.

I think of the late Robert A. Laidlaw, well-known businessman of Auckland, New Zealand and author of *The Reason Why*. As a young man of eighteen-and-a-half, he made a covenant with God that he would give a tenth of all his earnings. Later, at the age of twenty-five, he decided to change that amount to fifty percent of all his earnings. God continued to multiply

---

[11]Philippians 4:11-12
[12]Philippians 4:19
[13]Luke 6:38

his resources until he was giving even more to the work of the Lord. Later, writing at the age of seventy, he could say: "I want to bear testimony that, in spiritual communion and in material things, God has blessed me one hundredfold, and has graciously entrusted to me a stewardship far beyond my expectations when, as a lad of eighteen, I gave God a definite portion of my wages."

The same could be related of William Colgate who joined a church in the city of New York. As a boy, he gave ten cents to the Lord's work out of every dollar he earned. As his business prospered he gave two-tenths, rising to five-tenths. Then when his children were educated he gave all his income to God.

Then we could mention God's prospering hand on men like Heinz, of "57 Varieties" fame; H. P. Crowell of Quaker Oats; Kraft, of Kraft Cheese, and many others. The fact that all Christians do not become famous does not alter the principle that God multiplies our actual resources when we learn how to give sacrificially to God and His work.

The names I have just mentioned are world-famous, but the history of Christian giving has demonstrated that there is none so poor that he cannot give. There was a woman with no money and too old to work. She began to pray, 'Teach me how to obtain. Give me someone to send out and support as a missionary.' Before her death she was supporting ninety-three missionaries. Another, a young clerk, gave up his mid-morning coffee and buns, buying tracts with the pennies thus saved and seeking, through these, to lead men to Christ. A husband, scarcely able to make ends meet, determined that not one penny of income would be spent until he and his wife saw to it that twenty-five cents out of every dollar were given to God. By the end of the month their business had so prospered that they increased their giving and gave a joyful testimony to their church concerning the seal that the Lord had set upon their faith and obedience.

Others have made a sliding scale of giving, steeply increasing as their incomes rose. Timing counts, too, so our obedience must be prompt. A businessman went to a missionary society with $280.00 toward sending a new recruit overseas, but he was told that he was too late as they had just canceled her passage for lack of the money. In tears he then confessed: 'God told me to give it some days ago, but I delayed.'

"We must not expect to be untested in this act of faith. The patriarch Job gave generously to God,[14] and to the poor; but for a time he was stripped of everything, though later he received it back again in richer measure. Then there are times when God may accept our gifts and lay them up as treasure in heaven, as He promised the rich young ruler. Some give just because they are asked, without thought as to the value of the cause; others give for secondary reasons, while some give from love of God and after careful thought."

So we would say in the words of another: "If you want to be rich, give; if you want to be poor, grasp! If you want abundance, scatter; if you want to be needy, hoard!"

And again:

A man there was, and some did count him mad:
The more he gave away, the more he had.

Selected

The Word of God supports this by saying: "There is that scattereth, and yet increaseth; and there is that withholdeth more than is meet, but it tendeth to poverty. The liberal soul shall be made fat: and he that watereth shall be watered also himself."[15]

But the third thing that follows from this enrichment of usefulness in giving is that *He motivates our spiritual responsibility* — "God is able to . . . increase the fruits of your righteousness." In other words, He

[14]Job 1:5
[15]Proverbs 11:24-25

motivates our giving and then uses the gifts with which He has blessed us to become the fruits of righteousness to others. Thus the people and causes to which we give are not only materially blessed, but *spiritually* blessed because our giving is the fruit of righteousness. This, in the highest sense, is sowing to the Spirit. It is one thing to dispense a gift; it is quite another to impart a spiritual blessing by the act of giving. We have all had experiences of this sort. There is a kind of giving which may have enriched materially, but left us dead spiritually; whereas there is another quality of stewardship which may not have been enriching materially, but has blessed us spiritually. God teach us the enrichment of usefulness in giving until "our very hearts o'erflow"!

This brings us to our last consideration:

THE ENRICHMENT OF THANKFULNESS IN GIVING

"Being enriched in every thing to all bountifulness, which causeth through us thanksgiving to God. . . . Thanks be unto God for his unspeakable gift." Thankfulness is the ultimate in all Christian stewardship. When God has so worked in our hearts that giving turns to worship, then we have truly experienced the grace of giving. There is no greater evidence of a Spirit-filled person than a praising Christian. When Paul exhorts the believers at Ephesus to "be filled with the Spirit,"[16] he adds immediately, "Giving thanks always for all things unto God."[17] And so the Bible makes it plain that there is no greater enrichment of the total human personality than the spirit of thankfulness. Let us remember that in one of the profoundest statements we find in the New Testament, the apostle tells us that God has "predestinated us . . . according to the good pleasure of his will, to the *praise* of

[16]Ephesians 5:18
[17]Ephesians 5:20

90

the glory of his grace."[18] So our chief occupation in heaven is going to be worship and praise to God.

In this passage the apostle makes it evident that the enrichment of thankfulness comes by way of the ministry of giving. Thus he concludes his great teaching in these two chapters on Christian stewardship with this high concept of thankfulness. He shows that this enrichment of thankfulness in giving *satisfies the soul* — "Being enriched in every good thing to all bountifulness, which causeth through us thanksgiving to God." There is nothing more satisfying in all the world than the God-given thankfulness which comes through our ability to enrich others. It is a level of thankfulness rarely found in Christians today, but it is part of God's purpose for His children. Just as His own heart was never satisfied until He had given His all to redeem mankind, so the true believer can never be truly satisfied until he reaches the point where living for others fills him with thanksgiving to God. Paul expresses this gratitude when he says: "I thank Christ Jesus our Lord, who hath enabled me, for that he counted me faithful, putting me into the ministry; who was before a blasphemer, and a persecutor, and injurious."[19] In other words, the supreme cause of his thanksgiving was that God delivered him from bigoted self-centeredness and religious cruelty to serve others to the glory of God.

But this enrichment of thankfulness in giving not only satisfies the soul but also *edifies the church* — "For the administration of this service not only supplieth the want of the saints, but is abundant also by many thanksgivings unto God; while by the experiment of this ministration they glorify God for your professed subjection unto the gospel of Christ, and for your liberal distribution unto them, and unto all men."

These two verses are quite remarkable in that they show how the enrichment of thankfulness in giving

---

18Ephesians 1:5-6
19I Timothy 1:12-13

teaches the church both to praise and to pray. Paul points out that the saints at Jerusalem would be inspired to praise God because of the evident working of the Gospel in the Corinthian church. One of the greatest problems in convincing Christians and, particularly unbelievers, of the reality of the Gospel is the fact that there is seldom any evidence of practical liberality. And so thankfulness through giving not only edifies the church in the ministry of praise, but in the ministry of prayer, for Paul goes right on to say, "And by their prayer for you, which long after you for the exceeding grace of God in you." Nothing develops the capacity for prayer in the life of Christians as does the spirit of thanksgiving. Wherever you find thankful people you will find praying people; and we might well add that praise and prayer are the outstanding marks of an edified church.

In the third place, I want you to observe that the enrichment of thankfulness in giving ultimately *magnifies the Lord* — "Thanks be unto God for his unspeakable gift." This is truly the climax to the whole subject of giving. With depth of insight Paul concludes his treatment of this subject of giving with this glorious doxology. What he is saying is that every time we give with thankfulness we only reflect the unspeakable act of God when He gave His only begotten Son for the salvation of men. Already the apostle has touched upon this profound subject by declaring, "Ye know the grace of our Lord Jesus Christ, that, though he was rich, yet for your sakes he became poor, that ye through his poverty might be rich."[20]

Here is divine giving at its highest and deepest. At its highest level we are lifted to the great concept of the unmerited favor of God in sending His Son from heaven's glory down to earth's gloom. At its deepest level we are introduced to the unutterable poverty to which our Lord descended. Paul is so careful about

---

[20] II Corinthians 8:9

this that he uses a Greek word which means "pauperism." In other words, the Lord Jesus became a pauper on this earth that we might be introduced to all the richness of His grace. Now, says Paul, whenever we give, remember that we are only reflecting the self-giving of God, and this should fill us with unspeakable thanksgiving to our Lord.

So we have seen what we mean by the enrichment of giving. It is hard to understand how any sensitive and reasonable Christian can hold back from all that God demands and deserves in the light of such teaching. Who among us does not long to live a life of fruitfulness, joyfulness, usefulness and thankfulness? But Paul maintains this cannot happen and will not happen until we know how to give, not only of ourselves and our service but also of our substance. Indeed, the more we have studied this subject, the more it has become apparent that *the true measure of yieldedness to the Lordship of Christ is the measure of our discipline and devotion in Christian stewardship.* We can talk until doomsday about being surrendered Christians, but we virtually lie until we give evidence of our surrender through our stewardship. And make no mistake about it, when we stand before the judgment seat of Christ to render an account of our stewardship, we will wish that we had given more, since it is inescapably true that "what we spend, we lose; what we keep will be left to others; what we give away will remain forever ours."

THE MAINTENANCE OF THE MINISTRY

SCRIPTURE READING

Let him that is taught in the word communicate unto him that teacheth in all good things.

Be not deceived; God is not mocked: for whatsoever a man soweth, that shall he also reap.

For he that soweth to his flesh shall of the flesh reap corruption; but he that soweth to the Spirit shall of the Spirit reap life everlasting.

And let us not be weary in well doing: for in due season we shall reap, if we faint not.

As we have therefore opportunity, let us do good unto all men, especially unto them who are of the household of faith.

Galatians 6:6-10

7

THE MAINTENANCE OF THE MINISTRY

These studies on *The Grace of Giving* would not be complete without a consideration of the subject of the maintenance of the ministry. Throughout the Bible this theme is thoroughly handled for those who have eyes to see and hearts to respond. The instruction in Old Testament times was that the priesthood should receive "all the tenth in Israel for an inheritance, for their service which they serve, even the service of the tabernacle of the congregation."[1] And whenever the Children of Israel failed to fulfill this command it was regarded as robbing God Himself; hence Jehovah's solemn words in Malachi's day, "Ye are cursed with a curse: for ye have robbed me."[2] When we come to the New Testament, the teaching on ministerial support is just as strong and clear. Sending forth His disciples for their first evangelistic crusade the Master said: "Provide neither gold, nor silver, nor brass in your purses; nor scrip for your journey, neither two coats, neither shoes, nor yet staves: for the workman is worthy of his meat."[3] Then in apostolic times Paul made it abundantly plain that "the Lord ordained that they which preach the gospel should live of the gospel."[4] And writing to Timothy, the same apostle reminds this young pastor that the Scriptures teach us that we should "not muzzle the

[1] Numbers 18:21
[2] Malachi 3:9
[3] Matthew 10:9-10
[4] I Corinthians 9:14

ox that treadeth out the corn. And, The laborer is worthy of his reward."[5]

There were times, of course, when Paul, and doubtless many of his colleagues, engaged in tentmaking and other means of support to avoid being chargeable to young churches,[6] or giving cause for offense to those who were weak in the faith.[7] Generally speaking, however, ministerial support was the rule of the churches and has continued to be so down through the centuries; thus we have such instruction as is set out before us in Galatians 6:6-10.

Before we deal with this passage in detail, however, it may be well to point out that ministerial support in most of our modern churches is on a salary basis. How this salary is determined largely depends on the spirituality or carnality of the congregation. If the people are instructed in the Word of God and understand the basis on which the pastors are to be recompensed, then all is well. On the other hand, if the policy is to hire a man at a bargain price, irrespective of what the Scriptures teach, then inevitably the church is out of favor with God and the ministry is harmed. God forgive those whose outlook is embodied in the prayer of a man who rose to his feet on one occasion and said, "Dear Lord, You keep this man humble and we will keep him poor."

But now let us turn to the verses before us and observe:

THE NATURE OF THIS MINISTERIAL SUPPORT

"Let him that is taught in the word communicate unto him that teacheth in all good things." Here we have one of the clearest treatments of this matter of ministerial support that we find anywhere in the Bible. It is important, therefore, that all who profit from

[5] I Timothy 5:18
[6] I Thessalonians 2:9
[7] I Corinthians 9:15

true evangelical preaching should give close attention to what the Spirit of God has to say, for this instruction is addressed not only to the members of a local church, but to all who are blessed by the exposition of the Scriptures, whether it be in conference centers, crusades, over radio and television, or through the printed page.

Paul is telling us that the nature of this ministerial support calls for *the recognition of the ministry of the Word* — "Let him that is taught in the word." It appears that even at this early date there was an organized system of teaching in the local churches that obligated believers to recognize those who were appointed and anointed to minister the truth of God. This is an all-important principle which is sadly ignored in many of our churches today, with consequent spiritual impoverishment.

Jesus was forever exhorting His disciples: "Take heed *what* ye hear";[8] and again: "Take heed therefore *how* ye hear."[9] Like a refrain throughout the great hymn of His ministry, He was repeatedly saying, "He that hath ears to hear, let him hear."[10] When we come to the epistles, we read such statements as these: "Let the prophets speak two or three, and let the other judge." And again: "If any man think himself to be a prophet, or spiritual, let him acknowledge that the things that I write unto you are the commandments of the Lord."[11] *Wherever there was a lack of such discernment of the true ministry of the Word, the Apostle Paul always lamented the fact.* Think of his words to the Corinthian church when he says: "And I, brethren, could not speak unto you as unto spiritual, but as unto carnal, even as unto babes in Christ. I have fed you with milk, and not with meat: for hitherto ye were not able to bear it, neither yet now

---

[8]Mark 4:24
[9]Luke 8:18
[10]Matthew 11:15; 13:9, 43
[11]I Corinthians 14:29, 37

are ye able."[12] The writer to the Hebrews says the same thing when he declares: "For when . . . ye ought to be teachers, ye have need that one teach you again which be the first principles of the oracles of God; and are become such as have need of milk, and not of strong meat. For every one that useth milk is unskillful in the word of righteousness: for he is a babe. But strong meat belongeth to them that are of full age, even those who by reason of use have their senses exercised to discern both good and evil."[13]

So whenever there is a true recognition of the ministry of the Word, there is also a corresponding responsibility not only to attend on that ministry but to support it.

This brings us to the second thought in the nature of this ministerial support, namely, *the recompense of the ministers of the Word* — "Let him that is taught in the word communicate unto him that teacheth in all good things." As we have pointed out already, there was, at this early period of church history, an organized system of instruction in the church, demanding not only the recognition but also the recompense of the preachers of God's truth. From the beginning the apostles warned the church that "it was not reason that they should leave the word of God, and serve tables," but rather that they should give themselves "continually to prayer and to the ministry of the word."[14] And so the teacher, pastor and evangelist were dependent on the material support of those who enjoyed their ministry.

Now Paul is very specific in what he has to say about this matter of recompense. He says: "Let him that is taught in the word communicate unto him that teacheth *in all good things.*" The phrase, "all good things," in this context means "worldly wealth." Twice over the expression is used in the gospels in connec-

[12]I Corinthians 3:1-2
[13]Hebrews 5:12-14
[14]Acts 6:2, 4

tion with rich people. The first time Luke employs the expression he is describing the rich farmer who pulled down his old barns and built greater in order to have room to bestow his fruits and his goods.[15] He uses the words again in the story of the rich man in hell, when Abraham said to him, "Son, remember that thou in thy lifetime receivedst *thy good things*"[16] (see also Rom. 15:26-27 and I Cor. 9:11), where *carnal things* are spoken of in a good sense).

The implication is absolutely clear. God has never intended His servants to exist as paupers, while those who are enriched by their ministry live as princes. Only as a man is relieved from the care of providing for his own livelihood can he give adequate time to prayer, meditation, study and his work of preaching and counseling. Thank God all churches are not as niggardly and stingy as some we know; but God have mercy upon the congregations who have driven their pastors to distraction and despair because of lack of ministerial support! The British paper, *The Daily Mail,* carried this headline a number of years ago: "The Rev. J. D. Allen, rector of Beaumont, Essex, is going to play a barrel organ to raise money for church funds." Can we imagine anything more unworthy of the high calling of a true minister of God?

The idea of poverty for the minister has been *wrongly* woven into Christian thought. We have been told that because Christ was born in a stable and lived as a poor man this is how His servants should subsist. But this is a false argument altogether. The greatest crime in history was the failure of men to recognize the ministry of Jesus and to recompense Him by receiving Him into their hearts and homes and giving Him of their best. Instead, it is recorded that "He came unto his own (Greek, "things"), and his own received him not."[17] What they did to the Master, men and women

[15]Luke 12:18
[16]Luke 16:25
[17]John 1:11

still do to preachers today! A minister has a right to expect a standard of living which is commensurate with his high and holy vocation. He has to be a leader in many areas of private and public life, and this cannot be done without compensating ministerial support. How seriously, therefore, we need to ponder this forgotten aspect of truth!

But with the nature of this ministerial support Paul proceeds to:

THE FAILURE OF THIS MINISTERIAL SUPPORT

"Be not deceived; God is not mocked: for whatsoever a man soweth, that shall he also reap." Understood in their context, these are searching words indeed! What Paul, in effect, is saying is that it is all very well to make large professions of love for the ministry and then fail to support it. Indeed, he proceeds to show that this failure to undergird the ministry in deed as well as in word is a matter of *personal deception* — "Be not deceived." Literally, this means "do not be led astray." A Christian's responsibility to the ministry has absolutely nothing to do with his own personal reactions to God's method of communication. Truth transcends the human channel, and for the sake of truth we should support the ministry, whatever we think of the "foolishness of preaching." This, of course, does not mean that a man who is not commending the Gospel should be tolerated; but assuming that the anointing of the Spirit is upon a preacher of the Word, then what he looks like and how he speaks must not necessarily affect what he says.

The carnal Christians were unimpressed with the preaching of the Apostle Paul. They said "his presence was weak" and "his speech contemptible,"[18] and so they were led astray in fulfilling their responsibilities to this mighty man of God. We live in a day when people are sadly deceived by personality pa-

[18]II Corinthians 10:10

102

rades, emotional appeals and enticing words of man's wisdom. Thus, when the solid teacher of eternal truth comes along, the average listener is bored, unimpressed and invariably fails to fulfill his solemn duty to support him.

But observe further that the failure of this ministerial support is due to *spiritual rebellion* — "Be not deceived; God is not mocked." Here is language which is deliberately used by Paul to point up an attitude of spiritual rebellion. Actually, the text reads: "Be not deceived; *you cannot turn up your nose at God.*" No words could better describe the attitude of some people to the content and challenge of preaching which God demands of every true minister of the Word.

It was not long ago that a friend of mine told me of a pastor who was taken to task by his officers. Cornering him in the vestry one Sunday morning they said, "Any more of that kind of teaching and you are out." Now, in this instance, I happened to know that this minister was not a liberal, or even a carnal preacher; on the contrary, he was a returned missionary from China who had worked with the Overseas Missionary Fellowship for many years. He had gone deep with God and had an unquestionable anointing upon his preaching; but members of his congregation did not want his message, and so they "turned up their noses at God."

When is the great reversal going to take place? When will Christians cease to support liberal or carnal preachers who only want to fill their churches for the sake of reputation? When are congregations going to support the word of the cross, the claims of Christ and, indeed, the whole counsel of God?

But there is an even more solemn aspect of this matter of failure in ministerial support. It not only reveals personal deception and spiritual rebellion but exposes *moral corruption* — "For whatsoever a man soweth, that shall he also reap. For he that soweth to his flesh shall of the flesh reap corruption." The surface interpretation of these words is that carnal spending will inevitably reap a carnal harvest. This is an unalterable law, and a man is a fool not to recognize it. But there is also another meaning which is inseparably linked with the apostle's general theme of ministerial support. When a congregation or an individual fails to support a spiritual ministry, in preference for a carnal ministry, the result will not only be loss at the judgment seat of Christ, but moral corruption in the life of the church here and now. This is the tragic story of many congregations in our land where so-called Christians are sowing to the flesh in supporting carnal ministries, with resultant pollution and rottenness. God have mercy, therefore, on individuals or groups of people who are sowing to the flesh by refusing to support the only quality of preaching which He honors and blesses!

So we see in unmistakable terms what Paul means by the failure of ministerial support. In the last analysis it comes right down to personal deception, spiritual rebellion and moral corruption. Let us see to it that we are not caught up in the stream of religious apostasy, lest we should be "condemned with the world."[19]

This brings us to the positive aspect of our subject:

THE PLEASURE OF THIS MINISTERIAL SUPPORT

"He that soweth to the Spirit shall of the Spirit reap life everlasting. And let us not be weary in well doing: for in due season we shall reap, if we faint not." Once again, this spiritual law is capable of much wider application than Paul has in mind in this particular passage; but let us remember that his initial theme is that of the maintenance of the ministry. So in a very real sense he is speaking here of the pleasure of ministerial support in a twofold way.

---

[19] I Corinthians 11:32

First, there is *the joy of personal stewardship* — "He that soweth to the Spirit shall of the Spirit reap life everlasting. And let us not be weary in well doing: for in due season we shall reap, if we faint not." To sow to the Spirit, in this immediate context, is obviously to support a spiritual ministry. And this has the double reward of adding to our spiritual capital, in terms of glory, honor and immortality in the life to come,[20] and speeding the cause of the Gospel to the far ends of the earth here and now. Indeed, as we have seen in these studies, nothing is more worthwhile than this kind of personal stewardship. Such a ministry of support is so vital and essential to the life of the church that Paul adds, "Let us not *be weary* in well doing." The verb he uses is expressive of physical exhaustion and of relaxed effort. It describes the spiritual and moral collapse which may be caused in Christian service through lack of sustained spiritual stewardship.

My father served the Lord for nearly thirty years in the jungles of Portuguese West Africa. Throughout that whole period he was never on salary. In fact, he had no guarantee from one month to another as to whether or not financial support would be forthcoming; but thank God, he never lacked! He not only maintained the overhead costs of a missionary program, but he also brought up a family of three sons. In later years, when in the home country, he discovered people scattered all over the British Isles and elsewhere who had sacrificed greatly to support his work on the foreign field. In almost every case these people had been blessed by his ministry but had chosen to remain anonymous and channel their gifts through the Echoes of Service office in England. If these people had not been *unwearied in well doing* what would have happened to a lonely missionary in the heart of Africa, without a salary and without a mailing list?

---

[20]Romans 2:7

The second pleasure in this ministerial support is *the joy of practical fellowship* — "As we have therefore opportunity, let us do good unto all men, especially unto them who are of the household of faith." That expressive phrase, "the household of faith," undoubtedly includes all who are in the family of God. But in this context Paul unquestionably has in mind servants of God, like himself, who were dependent not only on personal stewardship but also on practical fellowship for daily maintenance. So he says, "Let us *do good* unto all men, *especially . . . them who are of the household of faith.*" This practical fellowship is the complement of personal stewardship. The latter has to do with gifts and giving, while the former lays stress on deeds and doing. It is one thing to discharge our stewardship responsibility by signing a check, but quite another matter to involve ourselves in the ministry of hospitality.

Have you ever taken the trouble to study the subject of Christian hospitality in the New Testament? If not, then you have lost out immeasurably, not only on a vital aspect of truth, but on a most needed aspect of Christian service. Writing to the Romans, Paul follows that great passage on full surrender to the will of God with the words, "Distributing to the necessity of saints; given to hospitality."[21] Instructing Timothy on the qualifications of an elder, the apostle insists that he must be a man "of good behavior, given to hospitality."[22] Then Peter, in his exhortation to persecuted believers "scattered throughout Pontus, Galatia, Cappadocia, Asia, and Bithynia," says: "Use hospitality one to another without grudging."[23] But perhaps the most forceful words on this subject come from the pen of John, who commends the beloved Gaius for his hospitality and charity to traveling evangelists and preachers who had gone forth in the Savior's

[21]Romans 12:13
[22]I Timothy 3:2
[23]I Peter 1:1; 4:9

name "taking nothing of the Gentiles." Concerning all such John says: "We therefore ought to receive such, that we might be fellow helpers to the truth."[24] Practical fellowship means more than financial support: it includes the cup of cold water given in the Savior's name, a meal lovingly prepared, a bed for the night and a host of other expressions of sanctified human kindness which the Church of Jesus Christ so much needs.

A little while ago my wife and I were graciously invited to spend a few days with some friends. Even in the midst of a busy program we were able to accept the kind offer. What overwhelmed us completely, however, was the fact that not only was hospitality provided, and a greatly needed opportunity for quietness, rest and fellowship, but a parting letter was handed to us which read something like this: "Dear Friends, This is to let you know what a privilege it has been to have you with us and to assure you of our love and prayers." Attached to this letter was a check to cover all our traveling expenses! I can tell you we thanked God that such thoughtful people were still to be found in Christian circles today!

Here, then, is a great subject not often handled from the pulpit — and still less practiced in the pew — but, as we have seen, it is God's truth which we cannot ignore or rationalize, if we are to be men and women of God. The Holy Spirit's ministry in this age is to guide us into all truth,[25] and we dare not leave out any aspect of it if we mean to go all the way with God. So let us take to heart these words of the apostle and practice what he means by *the maintenance of the ministry,* both in our local churches and wherever we encounter the faithful preaching of the Word. And then "let us not be weary in *this* well doing: for in due season we shall reap, if we faint not."

With such eternal prospects in view, let me ask:

---

[24]III John 7-8
[25]John 16:13

Supposing today were your last day on earth,
The last mile of the journey you've trod,
After all of your struggles, how much are you
   worth?
How much could *you take* home to God?

Don't count as possessions your silver and gold,
For tomorrow you leave them behind;
And all that is yours to have and to hold
Are the blessings you've given mankind.

Just what have you done as you've journeyed
   along —
That was really and truly worthwhile?
Do you feel you've done good and returned it
   for wrong?
Could you look o'er your life with a smile?

Selected

CONCLUSION

SCRIPTURE READING

Will a man rob God? Yet ye have robbed me. But ye say, Wherein have we robbed thee? In tithes and offerings. Ye are cursed with a curse: for ye have robbed me, even this whole nation. Bring ye all the tithes into the storehouse, that there may be meat in mine house, and prove me now herewith, saith the Lord of hosts, if I will not open you the windows of heaven, and pour you out a blessing, that there shall not be room enough to receive it.

Malachi 3:8-10

Lay not up for yourselves treasures upon earth, where moth and rust doth corrupt, and where thieves break through and steal: but lay up for yourselves treasures in heaven, where neither moth nor rust doth corrupt, and where thieves do not break through nor steal: for where your treasure is, there will your heart be also.

Matthew 6:19-21

Sell that ye have, and give alms; provide yourselves bags which wax not old, a treasure in the heavens that faileth not, where no thief approacheth, neither moth corrupteth. For where your treasure is, there will your heart be also.

Luke 12:33-34

But they that will be rich fall into temptation and a snare, and into many foolish and hurtful lusts, which drown men in destruction and perdition. For the love of money is the root of all evil: which while some coveted after, they have erred from the faith, and pierced themselves through with many sorrows.

I Timothy 6:9-10

By him therefore let us offer the sacrifice of praise to God continually, that is, the fruit of our lips giving thanks to his name. But to do good and to communicate forget not: for with such sacrifices God is well pleased. .

Hebrews 13:15-16.

CONCLUSION

To use the words of Solomon, "Let us hear the conclusion of the whole matter."[1] In the preceding chapters, I have endeavored to expound some important aspects of *The Grace of Giving*. Now it only remains for me to summarize, simply and succinctly, the areas of truth that we have covered. I have in mind young people, especially, who have come to me on countless occasions asking for directives on how to motivate and manage their ministry of giving. So I purpose to zero in on what I shall call the dynamics and mechanics of giving.

THE DYNAMICS OF GIVING

If you have carefully read the Scripture passages that introduce this chapter you will recall Paul's warning that "they that will be rich fall into temptation and a snare, and into many foolish and hurtful lusts, which drown men in destruction and perdition. For the *love of money* is the root of all evil." In other words, the apostle is telling us that there is something alluring and attractive about money. Indeed, before we know it, we are *loving* money! What is important, however, is that this love of money can be either misdirected by the devil or redirected by the Lord. This comes out in the Sermon on the Mount where the Master declared: "Lay not up for yourselves treasures upon earth . . . but lay up for yourselves treasures in heaven . . . for where your treasure is, there will your heart be also." And the writer to the Hebrews reminds us that "to do good and to communicate (to share what you have with others, N.E.B.) forget not: for with

---
[1]Ecclesiastes 12:13

111

such sacrifices *God is well pleased.*" In these two statements we have what I have elected to term the *dynamics* of giving. They are the love of treasure in heaven and the love of pleasure on earth. Stating these dynamics in this form will help to fix them in our minds and, I trust, in our hearts as well!

There is, first of all, *the love of treasure in heaven.* Jesus said that "where your treasure is, there will your heart be also." Recall the setting of these words for a moment. Treasure or wealth, among the ancients, consisted in such things as clothes, gold, silver, gems, houses, lands, wine and oil. In fact, the term defined the abundance of *anything* that aided the ornamentation and comforts of life. With this in view, our Lord warned, "Lay not up for yourselves treasures upon earth, where moth and rust doth corrupt, and where thieves break through and steal." Employing these figures of speech, Jesus cautions us that to set our hearts (our love) on earthly treasures will ultimately dissatisfy and even despoil us; for moths will gnaw at our clothes; rust (or more accurately erosion) will ruin our gold, silver and grain, and thieves will burgle our homes. In other words, there are forces in this world which render impossible the hoarding of permanent treasures here upon earth.

How well you and I know this! Perhaps this explains why rich people are seldom *genuinely* happy or secure. "Millionaires who laugh," confessed Andrew Carnegie, "are rare." Sir Ernest Cassel, who spent vast fortunes for the benefit of mankind, a multimillionaire, the friend of kings and emperors, said to one of his visitors: "You may have all the money in the world, and yet be a lonely and sorrowing man. The light has gone out of my life. I live in this beautiful house, which I have furnished with all the luxury and wonder of art; but, believe me, I no longer value my millions."[2]

---

[2]*The Prairie Overcomer,* p. 226

On the other hand, our Savior advises: "Lay up for yourselves treasures in heaven . . . for where your treasure is, there will your heart be also." And what He means is crystal clear. In the parallel passage in Luke, "the treasure in the heavens" is spelled out as *almsgiving*. This is stewardship of time, talents and tithes in the cause of the Gospel, the good of man, and to the glory of God. Once your heart and mine are set on treasures in heaven, life and service become dynamic. This interprets to us the dynamism of the early church[3] and the altruism of the Apostle Paul.[4]

Dr. A. W. Tozer addressed himself to this concept of the heavenly treasures when he wrote: "It is one of the glories of the Christian religion that faith and love can transmute lower values into higher ones. Earthly possessions can be turned into heavenly treasures.

"It is like this: A twenty-dollar bill, useless in itself, can be transmuted into milk and eggs and fruit to feed hungry children. Physical and mental powers, valuable in themselves, can be transmuted into still higher values, such as a home and an education for a growing family. Human speech, a very gift of God to mankind, can become consolation for the bereaved or hope for the disconsolate, and it can rise higher and break into prayer and praise of the Most High God.

"As base a thing as money often is, it yet can be transmuted into everlasting treasure. It can be converted into food for the hungry and clothing for the poor; it can keep a missionary actively winning lost men to the light of the gospel and thus transmute itself into heavenly values.

"Any temporal possession can be turned into everlasting wealth. Whatever is given to Christ is immediately touched with immortality. Hosanna to God in the highest!"[5]

---

[3] Acts 2:42-47
[4] I Corinthians 7:30; II Corinthians 12:15
[5] Editorial, *The Alliance Witness* October 8, 1958

If our treasure is in heaven it is secure. What is more, such an investment awaits the day of rewarding dividends! The most important thing, however, is that our hearts become united instead of divided; for Jesus reminds us that where our treasure is, there will our hearts be also, and that no man can "serve God and mammon (money)."[6] Or to use the language of the saintly Alexander Maclaren, "If our hearts are in heaven, then heaven will be in our hearts, and here we shall know the joy and the peace that come from 'sitting in heavenly places in Christ Jesus,' even whilst on earth. There is no blessedness, no stable repose, no victorious independence of the buffets and blows of life, except this, that my heart is lifted above them all, and, I was going to say, is inhaled and sucked into the life of Jesus Christ. Then if my heart is where my treasure is, and *He is my treasure,* 'my life is hid with Christ in God.' "[7] Here, then, is the love of treasure in heaven.

But there is also *the love of pleasure on earth.* The Bible says: "To do good and to communicate (to share what you have with others, (N.E.B.) forget not: for with such sacrifices God is *well pleased*" (Heb. 13: 16; see also Phil. 4:18). If the love of treasure in heaven is the first dynamic of giving, then the love of pleasure on earth is the second dynamic. The love of pleasure on earth, for the dedicated Christian, is the desire to please God. You will remember that this was the consuming passion of our blessed Lord. He could say, "I do always those things that please him."[8] And Paul recalling this fact, could later write: "Even Christ pleased not himself."[9] No wonder the Father's voice from heaven was heard to say, "This is my beloved Son, in whom I am well pleased."[10]

---

[6]Matthew 6:24
[7]*Expositions of Holy Scripture,* Vol. VI, 1942. p. 309
[8]John 8:29
[9]Romans 15:3
[10]Matthew 3:17; 17:5

If I were to ask you to state the highest ambition of your life, what would be your answer? Surely your reply would be "to *please* my God." And you would be right! Now we have learned that one of the things that brings pleasure to the heart of God is sacrificial giving, for we are told that "with such sacrifices God is well pleased." Observe carefully that God is not only pleased, but *well pleased*. Once again, what a dynamic motivation for life and service here on earth! Let us see to it then that we "honor the Lord with (our) substance, and with the firstfruits of all (our) increase."[11]

THE MECHANICS OF GIVING

If we are clear on the dynamics of giving the mechanics will take care of themselves! This is because love always finds a way to give, regardless of circumstances or cost. But even in this matter of mechanics the Word of God is plain and practical.

The grace of giving concerns four areas of our income. First, there are *the tithes which God demands*. He says: "Bring ye all the tithes into the storehouse, that there may be meat in mine house, and prove me now herewith, saith the Lord of hosts, if I will not open you the windows of heaven, and pour you out a blessing, that there shall not be room enough to receive it" (Mal. 3:10). As we have noted previously in these studies, the tithe is a tenth of our income and, according to this verse in Malachi, God *demands* the tithe without any deductions. He declares: "Bring ye *all* the tithes." To do any less is to rob God.

Moreover, this basic principle of giving to God pervades the entire Bible. I have sought to make this clear in earlier chapters, but, by way of recapitulation, let us recall that before the giving of the law tithing represented *the principle of giving*.[12] In other

11Proverbs 3:9
12Genesis 14:17-24

words, like the principle of the Sabbath, God introduced into the universe this rule of thumb as a guide for all ages. After the giving of the law tithing represented *the precept of giving*.[13] With the coming of Christ tithing represented *the pattern of giving*. He could say: "Think not that I am come to destroy the law, or the prophets: I am not come to destroy, but to fulfill."[14] It is inconceivable that our Lord would have kept every other aspect of the law and overlooked such a matter as tithing. In every area of righteous living He was and is our supreme Example. Indeed, He referred to this matter of tithing again and again.[15] Even the writer to the Hebrews expressly states that tithing is a matter of fulfilling the law.[16] In the days of the apostles, tithing represented *the privilege of giving*. In his epistle to the Romans, Paul takes pains to attack what we call today "situation ethics," and shows that no one can know the indwelling life of the Spirit without fulfilling the righteousness of the law.[17] Then he says, "Love is the fulfilling of the law."[18] Indeed, that particular context needs to be studied for Paul is clearly upholding the demands of the law in terms of Christian living and giving.

While Christ has taken the condemnation and curse of the law, He has in no way abrogated the outliving of the law by the power of the Spirit. In the first-century church, it is obvious to any instructed Christian that tithing represented *the practice of giving*. When Paul writes, "Upon the first day of the week let every one of you lay by him in store, as God hath prospered him,"[19] he is surely referring to the biblical principle already enunciated in the Scriptures. As

---

[13]Deuteronomy 14:22; Nehemiah 10:38
[14]Matthew 5:17
[15]Matthew 23:23
[16]Hebrews 7:5
[17]Romans 8:2-4
[18]Romans 13:10
[19]I Corinthians 16:2

a matter of fact, scholars have pointed out that the word "store" in that verse has an undoubted allusion to the storehouse tithing of Malachi's day. Later, in the second epistle of Paul to the Corinthians,[20] Paul gives the ultimate word on this matter. He declares: "Every man according as he purposeth in his heart, so let him give." The operative phrase in that text reads, "as he purposeth in his heart," and it is evident that this is not left to an unenlightened conscience or an uninstructed heart.

God never leaves us to guess, when it comes to matters of faith and practice, so why should He abandon us to our own decisions and devices when it concerns one of the most important areas in the whole of human existence? Outside of eating, drinking, sleeping and playing, we spend the greater part of our lives earning money. The inescapable issue which follows this observation concerns the management of our money, once we have acquired it. It is at this point that God breaks in with those words of prior claim: "Bring ye *all* the tithes into the storehouse."

Secondly, there are *the offerings which God deserves*. In Malachi's day, the Lord had to rebuke His people for withholding the offerings as well as the tithes. The terms of censure were specific: "Ye have robbed me . . . in tithes and *offerings*." The offerings were the gifts that were brought to God, over and above the tithes. For you and me, these offerings represent our response of *love* for heavenly blessings. There are, for instance, the material blessings, such as an increase in salary, a successful business deal, or an unexpected financial windfall, and so on. Then there are, of course, the spiritual blessings, such as a fresh act of surrender, a new discovery of truth, a deepened experience of God's grace, or a prayerful resolve to underwrite an added responsibility in the area of stewardship. Whether material or spiritual

[20]II Corinthians 9:7

blessings, "every good gift and every perfect gift is from above, and cometh down from the Father of lights, with whom is no variableness, neither shadow of turning."[21]

When we render our tithes, we look up to the Throne of Divine Government and say: "O God, we acknowledge Thee to be the Ruler of the universe and, therefore, entitled to our tithes. We are grateful that in Thee, and in Thee alone, we live and move and have our being. Amen!" When we bring our offerings, we kneel in worship before the Throne of Divine Grace and pray: "Our Father, in response to Thy redeeming mercy, revealed in Jesus Christ, we bring the offerings of our sacrificial love and surrendered lives. Amen!"

Thirdly, there are *the expenses which God directs*. The Bible says: "Recompense to no man evil for evil. Provide things honest in the sight of all men."[22] And again: "Render therefore to all their dues: tribute to whom tribute is due; custom to whom custom; . . . Owe no man any thing."[23] These are pointed and practical words concerning our daily expenses. If our lives are truly yielded to God, our financial affairs will be handled with integrity and punctuality. With the directives that God has given us, we shall see to it that we never live beyond our ability to meet our monetary obligations. We shall avoid launching projects that cannot be underwritten with actual cash or other securities. Then, of course, we shall be very careful to file our income tax returns with honesty and prompt dispatch. God says, "Render . . . to all their dues" and this is final.

Fourthly, there are *the savings which God defends*. Citing an illustration from family life, Paul writes: "The children ought not to lay up for the parents,

[21]James 1:17
[22]Romans 12:17
[23]Romans 13:7-8

but the parents for the children";[24] and in another place he declares: "If any provide not for his own, and specially for those of his own house, he hath denied the faith, and is worse than an infidel."[25] In my pastoral counseling, I have found tragic breakdown in this area of money matters. Husbands have failed their wives, parents have cheated their children, and grown sons and daughters have neglected their widowed mothers or other dependents. Such shortcomings are soundly and solemnly condemned by the Word of God; in fact, such dereliction of duty is described as *worse than infidelity*.[26]

In the light of the foregoing, it is certainly biblical and practical that savings accounts be established and insurance policies be taken out to cover the needs of dependents, emergency requirements, funeral expenses, and so on. Such financial matters should be thoroughly discussed in every Christian household. With an open Bible and in the atmosphere of prayer tithes, offerings, expenses and savings should be surveyed in relation to personal, as well as general, income. Happy and healthy is the family that is united on these issues! But in the last analysis, everyone of us is responsible to God in time, and accountable to Him in eternity.[27]

The question which usually arises at this point is whether or not these mechanics of giving actually work out in practice. The answer may appear to be simplistic and dogmatic, but it is in the affirmative, nonetheless! What God expects us to attempt He also enables us to achieve; and committed Christians have proved this to be true throughout the rolling centuries. So let us take heart in knowing that the grace *of* giving is also the grace *for* giving.

---

[24]II Corinthians 12:14
[25]I Timothy 5:8
[26]I Timothy 5:8
[27]Galatians 6:2-10

God made the sun — it gives.
God made the moon — it gives.
God made the stars — they give.
God made the air — it gives.
God made the clouds — they give.
God made the earth — it gives.
God made the sea — it gives.
God made the trees — they give.
God made the flowers — they give.
God made the fowls — they give.
God made the beasts — they give.
God made man — he . . . ?

Selected

APPENDIX

APPENDIX

In chapter four on The Ethics of Giving, we pointed out that at the judgment seat of Christ we shall be examined for "the things done in (the) body.[1] We also remarked that "happy is the man who is his own executor" (see page 60). Now without distracting in any way from the importance of "giving while living," there is an aspect of stewardship which must not be omitted from a book on *The Grace of Giving*. It concerns The Last Will and Testament of every informed and dedicated Christian.

Great responsibility is laid upon us, as believers in Christ, to be faithful in the stewardship of all worldly goods committed into our trust.[2] This includes the "final disposition of our goods and adequate provision for our loved ones."[3] Undoubtedly, the best way to discharge so weighty an obligation is to have a valid Christian Will.

No one without a Will can have assurance that loved ones will receive the care that was intended. The law of intestacy follows prescribed legal procedures which rarely coincide with the true wishes of the one who dies intestate (without a Will). Thus not one penny of such an estate would go to any Christian agency for the spread of the Gospel. The law does not honor good intentions!

So we must not allow procrastination or neglect to fail God or bring loss to our families. We must pray earnestly about the final disposition of our estates, realizing that our final accounting is not to our families or friends, but to Him with whom we are going to

[1]II Corinthians 5:10
[2]I Corinthians 4:2
[3]Isaiah 38:1; I Corinthians 14:40

123

spend eternity. With this in mind, the following information is offered to all who desire the necessary data for the preparation of an effective Christian Will.

Preamble to a Christian Will

I, the undersigned, (NAME)   , of (CITY)   , in the County of   , and State of   , being of sound mind and disposing memory, realizing the uncertainty of this life, but with confidence in God and trust in His Son, Jesus Christ, my Lord, who died for my sins upon the cross, and rose again to justify me and give me eternal life, I do hereby make, publish and declare this to be my Last Will and Testament, and I hereby will and dispose of all the property of which I am the owner at my death in the following manner.

Such a Preamble to a Christian Will is important when it is recognized that this document, more often than not, is read in the presence of unbelievers.

Distribution of Estate

I. **Specific Bequests and Devises:**
   a. This portion of the Will contains bequests of a specific nature, such as gifts of personal property (called "legacies") or of real estate (called "devises").
   b. Items of considerable value (such as a rare painting, an expensive diamond ring, or a collection of valuable objects) should be included in the Will, unless they are to be sold and their value added to the main body of the estate. In every case the property should be so described as to be readily identified.
   c. A Will is of no effect until the death of the Testator who makes it. In most states a gift fails if the donee dies before the Testator, unless the donee is a close relative and has living

descendents. A substitute donee might be named for each bequest; otherwise, the Will should be revised upon the death of an important donee. A failure of a gift usually amounts to the revocation of that part of the Will only, the designated sum reverting to the residue of the estate.

II. Bequests to Christian Agencies:

a. For most Christians, the Will provides an opportunity to make a final gift to the cause of Christ substantially larger than that which is possible during life. It should be considered the climax of a life of Christian stewardship and testimony.

b. Agencies should be selected with utmost caution, in respect to doctrine, leadership, financial competence, successful service and high ethics. With scores of worthy and highly reputable agencies in need of funds, it is a tragedy that so much of the Lord's money is passed on to unsound or irresponsible agencies.

c. In the case of benevolent organizations, it is important that the full legal name and address be given.

d. Gifts may be in the form of trusts, a specific amount of cash, real estate or securities, or percentage of the total estate.

III. Residue of Estate:

a. Ordinarily, the body of the Will consists of a number of specific bequests and devises, followed last of all by the "residual clause." Contrary to what the name seems to imply, the residuary section of the Will frequently distributes the bulk of the Testator's estate. There is a reason for this. Specific gifts may be disturbed by changes in the Testator's estate before death; values alter in ways unforeseen; a beneficiary may die, and the gift which has lapsed be added to the residue. Hence, the principal beneficiaries normally "take" under the residuary clause.

b. Because of the extreme uncertainty concerning the final size of the estate, this portion is normally divided by means of percentages.

IV. Appointment of Guardian:

a. Under normal circumstances, the surviving spouse is named the guardian of minor children. It is essential that this be included in the Will to avoid the necessity of court appointment and the cost of bonds and legal fees.

b. In the event both parents should become deceased, an alternate guardian should be named; otherwise the choice would be thrown back on the discretion of the court.

c. Unless otherwise specified, the guardian cares for both the person and the estate of the minor child. If a bequest is not to be granted until the child reaches majority, or is emancipated by marriage or military service, the Executor may be directed to make such payment.

V. Appointment of Executor:
(feminine, Exccutrix)

a. The Executor is the personal representative of the deceased, appointed by him with legal authority to discharge his liabilities, execute his contracts, recover all things due his estate, and carry his Will into effect.

b. A near relative or a close friend may not always be the best choice to act as Executor. Qualifications include business ability, impartiality, and probable availability. It may be advisable to appoint a professional Executor — a bank or trust company.

c. If a relative or friend is named, it is frequently advisable to name a joint executor or an alternate executor, and to specify that they should serve "without bond."

d. Should a person die without a legal Will, the court appoints an Administrator to finalize the affairs of the deceased and to distribute his estate. Such a one looks for direction only to the laws of the state, which may be in serious conflict with the wishes and intentions of the deceased. Bonds and legal fees may unnecessarily shrink the estate. Obviously, a well-written, effective Christian Will is the answer.

VI. **Appointment of Trustee:**

a. When a trust is to be established in a Will, it is necessary to name a Trustee to carry out the desires of the Testator. It is recommended that a bank or trust company be named together with a trusted individual. This will provide competency and understanding.

b. The Trustee is empowered to do all things necessary and convenient for the investment and reinvestment of any part of the estate that is left in trust. He will manage and control the corpus of the trust and pay out of the same as provided in the Will, or, in the absence of same, by statute or rules of law regulating investments of Trustee.

ESTATE PLANNING INFORMATION

A. PERSONAL:

1. Name _____
   Known By Other Names _____
   Address _____
   Telephone _____
2. Date of Birth _____
3. Place of Birth _____
4. Have Birth Certificate? _____
5. Location _____

6. Citizen of _____
7. Citizenship acquired by: Birth _____
                             Naturalization _____
                             Marriage _____
8. Location of Citizenship Papers _____
9. Social Security Number _____
10. Location _____
11. Passport # _____
12. Issue Date _____
13. Issued at _____
14. Location _____
15. Military Service:
         Nation Served _____
         Dates of Service _____
         Branch _____
         Grade_____ Serial #_____
         Location of Discharge Papers _____
         Service-connected Benefits _____
         Service-connected Disability _____
         Claim # _____
         Military Honors or Decorations _____
         Location of Above _____
16. Marital Status:
         Single _____
         Married _____
         Divorced _____
         Separated _____
         Widow(er) _____
17. Name of Spouse _____
18. Date and Place of Marriage _____
19. Location of Marriage Certificate _____
20. Previous Marriages _____
21. How Terminated _____
22. Location of Termination Papers _____

B. FAMILY INFORMATION

1. Father's Full Name _____
2. Mother's Maiden Name _____

3. Children —
  Name   Birth Date

4. Grandchildren —
  Name   Birth Date

5. Brothers and Sisters —
  Name   Birth Date

C. EMPLOYMENT:

1. Employer _____
2. Address _____
3. Benefit Plans —
  Insurance _____
  Pension _____
  Profit Sharing _____
  Other Benefits _____

D. ASSETS:

Name of Bank _____
Address _____
Type of Account _____ Amount _____
Insurance:
Name of Company _____
Beneficiary _____
Type of Policy _____ Amount _____
Bonds
Stocks
Broker
Real Property
Mortgages
Other Property
Safe Deposit Box
Debts
Income Tax Records
Trusts
  Trustee _____
  Location of Trust Agreement _____

E. CEMETERY PLOT:

Have _____
Cemetery Name _____
        Section _____ Plot _____
Perpetual Care _____
Location of Deed _____
Funeral Preference —

F. WILL:

1. Specific Bequests and Devises

Name and Address	Description of Gift

2. Bequests to Christian Agencies

		_____%
Legal Name	Address	Amount

3. Need of a Trust

_____
_____

4. Residue of Estate

	_____%
Name and Address	Amount

5. Appointment of Guardian and Alternate
   Guardian

Name	Address
To Be Bonded? _____	
Alternate	

Name	Address

6. Appointment of Executor and Alternate Executor

_____   _____
Name   Address
        To Be Bonded? _____
Alternate

_____
Name   Address
7. Appointment of Trustee
Trustee

_____   _____
Name   Address
        To Be Bonded? _____
Alternate

_____
Name   Address

Signature _____   _____
        Name   Address
Telephone No. _____
                            City   State   Zip
Date _____

131

REFERENCES

In our study of *The Grace of Giving,* we have primarily focused our attention on the Corinthian letters for reasons already given (see Introduction). The subject of stewardship, however, has a far wider mention and treatment in the Bible; and the Christian who desires to know "the whole counsel of God" on this important doctrine should examine carefully both Old and New Testaments. To initiate and assist such seekers after truth, the following outline and references are prayerfully offered. It is hardly necessary to add that the material is suggestive rather than exhaustive. A good concordance, a Treasury of Scripture Knowledge, and a close following of cross-references will aid further research.

THE STANDARD OF GIVING

The Tithes
Genesis 14:20; 28:22; Leviticus 27:30-33; Numbers 18:21-32; Deuteronomy 12:5-19; 14:22-29; 26:12-15; II Chronicles 31:5-6, 12; Nehemiah 10:37-38; 12:44; 13:5, 12; Proverbs 3:9; Ezekiel 45:11; Amos 4:4; Malachi 3:8-10; Matthew 23:23; Luke 11:42; 18:12; Hebrews 7:2, 4, 8-9, etc.

The Offerings
Exodus 30:14-15; 35:4-29; Numbers 31:52; I Chronicles 29:6-17; II Chronicles 31:10-14; Ezra 1:6; 2:68; 3:5; 7:15-16; Nehemiah 10:37-39; 13:5; Malachi 3:8; Hebrews 5:1, 3; 8:4, etc.

The Sacrifices
Philippians 4:18; Hebrews 13:15-16, etc.

Collections

II Chronicles 24:6; Acts 11:29 (Relief); Romans 15:26 (Contribution); I Corinthians 16:1, etc.

THE SUBSTANCE OF GIVING

Increase

Deuteronomy 14:22-28; 26:12; II Chronicles 31:5; Proverbs 3:9, etc.

Riches

I Chronicles 29:1-22; Psalm 112:3; Ecclesiastes 5:19; Jeremiah 9:23-24; II Corinthians 8:2; Revelation 5:12, etc.

Treasures

Joshua 6:19-24 (Treasury); I Chronicles 9:26; 28:12; II Chronicles 32:27; Nehemiah 7:68-72; 10:38-39; 13:12-13; Proverbs 15:6; Matthew 6:19-21; 19:21; Mark 10:21; 12:41, 43; Luke 12:33-34; 18:22; 21:1, John 8:20, etc.

Good(s)

Deuteronomy 6:6-25; Mark 14:6; Luke 11:13; 16:25; Acts 9:36; Galatians 6:6-10; Hebrews 10:24; 13:16; I Peter 4:10; I John 3:17, etc.

Gifts

Genesis 25:6; Exodus 28:38; Leviticus 23:38; Numbers 18:6-29; Psalm 72:10; Proverbs 19:6; Matthew 2:11; 5:23-24; 8:4; 23:18-19; Philippians 4:17; Hebrews 5:1; 8:3-4; 9:9, etc.

Money

Exodus 30:16; II Chronicles 24:5-14; 34:9-14; Ezra 3:7; Matthew 22:19; 25:18, 27; Mark 12:41; Luke 19:12-27; Acts 4:37, etc.

Possessions

Matthew 19:22; Acts 2:45; 4:34; 5:1, etc.

Wealth

Deuteronomy 8:17-18; Ruth 2:1; II Chronicles 1:

11-12; Psalm 112:3; Proverbs 10:15; 19:4; Ecclesiastes 5:19, etc.

THE SPIRIT OF GIVING

Liberality
Deuteronomy 15:12-15; Proverbs 11:24-26; I Corinthians 16:3; II Corinthians 8:2; 9:13, etc.

Charity
Matthew 22:37-39; I Corinthians 13:3; II Corinthians 8:7-8, 24 (Love); I Thessalonians 1:3; 3:6; Hebrews 6:10; 10:24; I John 3:16-17; III John 6; Revelation 2:19, etc.

Hilarity
Ezra 6:15-18; II Corinthians 8:2 (Joy); 9:7 (Cheerfulness), etc.

Hospitality
Romans 12:13; I Timothy 3:2; Titus 1:8; Hebrews 13:1-2; I Peter 4:9, etc.

THE SECRET OF GIVING

Giving
Genesis 25:6; Exodus 30:12-15; Leviticus 23:10, 38; Deuteronomy 10:18; Psalm 72:10-11; Matthew 10:8; Luke 11:41; Acts 20:35, etc.

Scattering
Proverbs 11:24, etc.

Sowing
II Corinthians 9:6-10; Galatians 6:7-8, etc.

Communicating
II Corinthians 8:4; Galatians 2:2; 6:6 (Showing Fellowship); Philippians 1:5; 4:14-15; I Timothy 6:18; Philemon 6; Hebrews 13:16; III John 8, etc.

THE SYSTEM OF GIVING

The Where of Giving
"Now concerning the collection . . . I have given order to *the churches*" (I Corinthians 16:1).

The When of Giving
"Upon *the first day of the week*" (I Corinthians 16: 2).

The Who of Giving
"Let *every one of you*" (I Corinthians 16:2).

The What of Giving
"Let every one of you *lay by him in store,* as God hath prospered him . . . every man according as he purposeth in his heart . . . not grudgingly, or of necessity" (I Corinthians 16:2; II Corinthians 9:7).

The Why of Giving
"God loveth a cheerful giver" (II Corinthians 9: 7).

THE SERVICE OF GIVING

Giving Supports the Weak of the Church
Acts 2:44-47; 4:32-37; *20:35;* II Corinthians 8: 1-24; II Corinthians 9:1-15, etc.

Giving Sustains the Work of the Church
I Corinthians 9:9-14; Galatians 6:6-10; Philippians 1:5; 4:14-15; Hebrews 6:10, etc.

A critical examination of the foregoing references will reveal that, in many instances, *one* English word is employed to express a variety of Hebrew or Greek terms in the Old and New Testaments respectively. For example, the word "tithe" or "tithing" in the original texts have different shades of meaning not apparent in our English translations. This fact, however, only serves to enrich and enforce the doctrine of *The Grace of Giving.* Let us then read, learn, mark and inwardly digest what God has to say on this subject until knowledge becomes *action.*

BIBLIOGRAPHY

ARTICLES

Dark, Alvin. "Why I Tithe." *The American Weekly.*

Macaulay, J. C. "Men Ought to Give." *L.B.I. News,* May, 1961.

Olford, Stephen F. "The Lord's Treasury." *American Tract Society,* 1964.

Panton, D. M. "Laying Up Treasure." *The Prairie Overcomer,* pp. 225-228, June, 1964.

Pritchard, R. H. "Giving." *Harvester,* April, 1938.

BOOKLETS

Buxton, B. Godfrey. *Stewardship.* London, The Fellowship of Interdenominational Missionary Societies.

Keyes, Kenneth S. *In Partnership with God.* Miami, The Keyes Foundation.

Laidlaw, Robert A. *Giving to God,* 3d ed. London, Living Waters Missionary Union.

Rees, Tom. *Money Talks.* Sevenoaks, Kent, England, Hildenborough Hall.

BOOKS

Barclay, William. *The Letters to the Corinthians.* Edinburgh, The Saint Andrew Press.

――――. *The Letters to the Galatians and Ephesians.* Edinburgh, The Saint Andrew Press.

CSSM Choruses (No. 1). London, Children's Special Service Mission.

DeHaan, M. R. *Galatians.* Grand Rapids, Radio Bible Class.

Hobbs, Herschel. *The Epistles to the Corinthians.* Grand Rapids, Baker Book House, 1960.

Hodge, Charles. *II Corinthians.* New York, A. C. Armstrong & Son, 1891.

Ironside, H. A. *Second Epistle to the Corinthians*. Neptune, Loizeaux Brothers.

Kelly, William. *Notes on Corinthians*. London, G. Morrish, 1878.

Laurin, Roy L. *Second Corinthians*. Findlay, Dunham Publishing Co.

Morgan, G. Campbell. *The Corinthian Letters of Paul*. Old Tappan, Fleming H. Revell Co.

Naismith, A. *1200 Notes, Quotes and Anecdotes*. London, Pickering & Inglis Ltd., 1962.

Ockenga, Harold. *The Comfort of God*. Old Tappan, Fleming H. Revell Co.

Redpath, Alan. *Blessings Out of Buffetings*. Old Tappan, Fleming H. Revell Co., 1965.

--------------. *The Royal Route to Heaven*. Old Tappan, Fleming H. Revell Co., 1960.

Tasker, R. V. G. *II Corinthians*. Grand Rapids, Wm. B. Eerdmans Pub. Co., 1958.

Warren, M. A. C. *The Gospel of Victory*. London, SCM Press Ltd.

Worship and Service Hymnal. Chicago, Hope Publishing Company, 1960.

Wuest, Kenneth S. *Galatians in the Greek New Testament*. Grand Rapids, Wm. B. Eerdmans Pub. Co.

COMMENTARIES

Eadie, John. *Commentary on the Epistle of Paul to the Galatians*. Grand Rapids, Zondervan Publishing House.

Ellicott's Commentary on the Whole Bible. Vol. VII-VIII, Acts to Revelation. Grand Rapids, Zondervan Publishing House, 1959.

Harrison, Everett F., and Pfeiffer, Charles F. *The Wycliffe Bible Commentary*. Chicago, Moody Press.

Luther, Martin. *Commentary on St. Paul's Epistle to the Galatians*: A New Abridged Translation by Theodore Graebner. Grand Rapids, Zondervan Publishing House.

The New Bible Commentary. Grand Rapids, Wm. B. Eerdmans Pub. Co., 1956.